I0139835

BLACK FOREST

Anthony Giardina

BROADWAY PLAY PUBLISHING INC
New York
www.broadwayplaypublishing.com
info@broadwayplaypublishing.com

Cover art compliments of the Long Wharf Theatre

First printing: December 2008
I S B N: 978-0-88145-395-9

Book design: Marie Donovan
Word processing: Microsoft Word
Typographic controls: Ventura Publisher
Typeface: Palatino
Printed and bound in the U S A

CHARACTERS & SETTING

JACOB FREUNDLICH, *early to mid forties, Associate Professor of English*

WENDY CUNNINGHAM, *twenty-one, Senior English major; African American*

MARGARET OLIN, *late thirties, Associate Professor of English*

FRANK LEECH, *early to mid sixties, Professor of English*

CHRIS MACADEN, *mid thirties, Assistant Professor of English*

HOMER BOYKIN, *mid to late sixties, Professor of English*

AARON GOLDMAN, *late forties, Professor of English*

HEIDI LEECH, *early sixties,* FRANK's *wife*

LEAH FREUNDLICH, *early forties,* JACOB's *wife*

NICOLE GOLDMAN, *mid to late forties,* AARON's *wife; French*

The play takes place at and around one of the last surviving women's colleges, just at the end of the 20th century.

An earlier version of BLACK FOREST was presented at Seattle Repertory Theater in 1994, directed by Doug Hughes.

The play had its premiere at the Long Wharf Theater in New Haven on 20 March 2000. The cast and creative contributors were

JACOB FREUNDLICH . . . . Reed Birney
WENDY CUNNINGHAM . . . . Kim Awon
MARGARET OLIN . . . . Sharon Scruggs
FRANK LEECH . . . . Jack Ryland
CHRIS MACADEN . . . . Dave Simonds
HOMER BOYKIN . . . . Ron Parady
AARON GOLDMAN . . . . Tom Tammi
HEIDI LEECH . . . . Jennifer Harmon
LEAH FREUNDLICH . . . . Laura Hughes
NICOLE GOLDMAN . . . . .Patricia Hodges

Director . . . . Doug Hughes
Original music . . . . Paul Sullivan
Set design . . . . .Hugh Landwehr
Costume design . . . . Jess Goldstein
Lighting design . . . . Michael Chybowski
Sound design . . . . .Matthew Mezick
Dialect coach . . . . Gillian Lane-Plescia
Production stage manager . . . . .Kevin E Thompson
Casting . . . . Bernard Telsey Casting

ACT ONE

Scene One

(JACOB FREUNDLICH's *office*)

(JACOB *is talking to* WENDY CUNNINGHAM, *a black student who has come to discuss a proposed Independent with him. He sits at one of two desks in the room [*JACOB *shares his office with another Professor]. Between the two desks are a pair of very tall windows which open outward, facing stage right. Below the windows is a window seat.* JACOB's *office-mate's desk faces upstage, and* JACOB's *downstage, facing the audience.* WENDY *is seated in a chair next to* JACOB's *desk.*)

WENDY: It's called "Black Forest". That is, I want to call it "Black Forest". Schnitzler, you know, said the soul— the human soul—is an undiscovered country.

(JACOB *stares at her a moment, then tries to open a stuck drawer.*)

WENDY: And I think that's really true. I mean, after Freud, after all we think we know about ourselves, we still don't really have a *clue.*

(JACOB's *still pulling at the door, having trouble.*)

WENDY: I hope this doesn't sound incredibly—

JACOB: No.

WENDY: —*stupid.* Or naïve. I try to put together ideas sometimes, I'll work for a week or a month, I'll come up with something finally and show it to someone. They say, "Well, isn't that kind of obvious?"

JACOB: *(Having given up on the drawer)* You shouldn't think that way. Go on.

WENDY: Don't you want to—open the drawer?

JACOB: It was nothing. No.

WENDY: *(Beat)* Well, my thesis—I mean, if you agreed to work with me on an Independent this semester—would be—*proving* that, sort of. Or proving, at least, that this is the content of Eastern European literature in this century. I got this from your classes, so don't laugh.

JACOB: I'm not laughing.

WENDY: That, well, first, two centuries ago, a century ago, there was just this very limited notion of the self. Then, in the twentieth century, we embraced this concept, and suddenly there's nothing else. Wars, famines, who cares? The ultimate goal is to know ourselves. In America we're obsessed with it—the best seller list is loaded down with books that supposedly give us the shortcuts to the soul—and in all this time, in Europe, at least from Kafka on, there's been this chorus of guys, *laughing* at us— "You think there's such a thing as the self."

(A silence. JACOB *looks at* WENDY. *She becomes sheepish.)*

WENDY: I'm sorry, is it—dumb?

JACOB: No. It's entirely viable. I'm just not the man for it.

WENDY: But you—I mean, it was in your classes—

JACOB: There's a man down the hall. He's very good. Frank Leech.

WENDY: I know Professor Leech. He's 19th Century Poetry, isn't he?

JACOB: Please don't take offense. I'm going to be frank with you. I'm going to respect your intelligence and—maturity. I'm sick of Kafka. I can't read him anymore. I know that everything he and his progeny have to say is enormously important, but frankly, at this point in my life, I'm more inclined to go with the best-seller list. *(Beat)* I'm not trying to make easy jokes at your expense, please don't think that. The thought of sitting here, for an entire semester, dealing with the unknowability of things—is that *really* what you want to do?

WENDY: You probably don't remember me from the classes I took with you. Three of them. I'm quiet, usually. I sit in the back. I declared an English major and then I threw up—I mean, the audacity. People like me are supposed to go into Education, Social Sciences —but something you said, you probably don't even remember.

JACOB: *(Beat)* I don't, no.

WENDY: We were finishing a whole section on Kafka. And some of us, not me, some of the others in the class, felt unhappy, depressed, like what's the point, and you said, very gently, you sat on your desk and came close to us and said, In one age, Dante was representative; in another, Shakespeare—

JACOB: It wasn't original. I was quoting.

WENDY: And those ages were lucky, in a way, you said, to live in a world reflected accurately by that kind of writing. But our age, like it or not, is most accurately represented by another kind of writer. A Jew. An isolated man. Terribly lonely. Incapable of significant action. *(Beat)* We don't have to love that world, you said. But we do have to recognize it's the one we live in. *(Beat)* I'm taking up too much of your time. *(She starts to gather her books.)*

JACOB: *(Still reacting thoughtfully to what she's just said)* I'll be happy to write you a note for—

WENDY: It's not Kafka. Not him you're sick of. Not you. *(Quite brave now)* I couldn't help but notice, in the last class I took with you, you didn't care so much. You let us all sort of—flounder. Usually, you would have stepped in and explained it to us all, in a way that— made sense. And I couldn't help but wonder, did something happen to you?

(Beat. JACOB wants to tell WENDY. But he backs off, finishes the note he's been writing.)

WENDY: I'm sorry. Excuse my presumption. I'll talk to Professor Leech.

(JACOB finishes the note, holds it out, not yet offering it.)

JACOB: *Three* classes you took with me.

WENDY: I hardly said anything. I sat in the back.

(JACOB hands WENDY the note. She takes it, exits. As soon as she's gone, he reaches out, a small, aborted gesture, as if he'd like to keep her there. He can't. The phone rings.)

JACOB: Hello. *(Wearily)* Yes, yes, I know, Juliana's piano lesson's at three-thirty. *(Beat)* Okay, give it to me. *(Searching for a pencil on his mess of a desk)* What? No. Go ahead. Soccer? They want me to coach? *(His initial pleasure turning to disappointment:)* Assistant coach. What'd you—you already told them? You said I would?

(A knock at the door.)

JACOB: Come in.

(MARGARET OLIN enters. A woman roughly JACOB's age, very attractive, dressed in post-hippie chic, and, at the moment, totally distraught. JACOB doesn't notice the state she's in. He gestures for her to sit down, then resumes the phone conversation with his wife.)

JACOB: Did you consider the time commitment?
Volunteering to coach children's sports is like entering
the convent, Leah. Everything else you renounce.
(Beat) It's no one. No one. You thought it would be
good for me? Engagement. Thank you very much
but hold on, you don't have the right to—

(While JACOB *hasn't been paying attention,* MARGARET
*has plopped herself down in the chair formerly occupied
by* WENDY, *and begun crying. Finally,* JACOB *notices.)*

JACOB: Someone, seems to be crying in my office, Leah.
No, it's not a student. I'll call you back. *(He hangs up.
Stares a moment at* MARGARET. *Not immediately solicitous)*
What is it?

MARGARET: Nothing.

JACOB: Don't cry and tell me nothing. Come on.

MARGARET: You're the only one I could come to.
I am so humiliated. The *shit*.

JACOB: What? What shit?

MARGARET: Aaron.

JACOB: Aaron Goldman? Our Chairman? What did he
do?

MARGARET: Dumped me. The shit.

JACOB: *(This last takes it, for him, to a lower level of
seriousness.)* I love this—the most articulate people in
the world, faced with an actual emotion, reduced to the
language of caca. Where did he dump you? When?

MARGARET: Just now. Over in Dickinson's. Can you
understand? If you're going to dump somebody, fine.
But you don't tell someone it's over, that you are seeing
someone else, on the first day of classes, in a crowded
restaurant, full of students, where I have to go into the
ladies room and crawl into a stall just so I can cry.

(Beat. JACOB *has no response.)*

MARGARET: What? What are you thinking?

JACOB: Nothing. It's unworthy of me. It's just, I was thinking, there's got to be something really wrong with a society that names so many things after Emily Dickinson.

MARGARET: *(Getting up as if to leave)* I can see I'm not going to get any sympathy here.

JACOB: I told you Aaron Goldman was a shit from the day you started going out with him.

MARGARET: *(Not budging)* Yes, that's true.

JACOB: Any man who invites another man to play tennis with him just so they can take a shower together is not a good bet as a lover.

MARGARET: Yes, I've heard the rumors. And I have to say there was no evidence of that, all right? All I know is right now I'd like to punish him.

JACOB: Revenge on Aaron Goldman? Come on, it only matters if you loved him.

MARGARET: Oh, please, *love* is not even a consideration here. *Love.* You're an old fashioned romantic. You've been married since the Dark Ages, so you don't see that a whole level of intimacy exists now, between people, *outside* of love, that can just as seriously be betrayed.

*(*JACOB *just gives her a questioning look, raising his eyebrows, suggesting he doesn't believe a word of what she's just said.)*

MARGARET: All right, forget it, I should have gone to someone else.

JACOB: Frank Leech. Down the hall. He'd have given you a grade. I at least listen.

MARGARET: Is that what this is called?

JACOB: I'm just so disappointed. How can smart women fall for such apes?

MARGARET: *(Giving him a very ambiguous look)* That really is none of your business.

JACOB: Oh, so he was good in bed. Thank you very much, I don't want to hear about this. Me with my three children and my kind little wife. I do not want to hear about the bedroom acrobatics of Aaron Goldman.

MARGARET: I didn't say that, did I?

JACOB: *(Looking off, going into a riff of his own)* And why shouldn't he be good in bed? Christ, he's been married to Simone Signoret for twenty years. All that Gallic regret, of course she taught him a thing or two in the sack.

MARGARET: Let me know when you're ready to talk about me, all right? Goddamn you.

JACOB: *(Going to her apologetically, leading her to a seat)* I'm sorry. It's the brain, it's what starts happening when you reach forty.

MARGARET: Maybe if you were *doing* something, instead of sitting here day after day—

JACOB: *(Interrupting)* Yes, yes, doing something, that would do the trick, wouldn't it?

MARGARET: You haven't done a book in—what? —eight years?

JACOB: For which I should be congratulated. Have you seen the latest catalogue from Routledge? How many more times are we going to have to traipse into the kitchen of Sylvia Plath's dreary flat tracing the path of her head into the oven so that we can better appreciate a few third rate—

MARGARET: *(Overlapping on "a few third rate")* Better to die, I suppose.

JACOB: *(A little more serious than expected)* I'm not dead.
(Beat) Not yet. I just don't care so passionately to run
this particular race. I've got two books—

MARGARET: Oh, shut up.

(FRANK LEECH *enters, holding a sheet of paper, the note*
JACOB *gave to* WENDY *earlier.* FRANK *is very tall,
very dignified, and though he was born in New York City,
very English.)*

FRANK: Jacob— *(He notices* MARGARET. *There's disdain
for her even in this moment's recognition. He's pretty good
at masking it, though.)* Oh. Excuse me. About this student
you sent me. Shall I come back?

JACOB: Would you? We're— *(Apologetic)* This is private.

FRANK: Oh, sure. *(Regarding the door:)* Leave it open?
A crack? In case a student comes by?

JACOB: Oh. Gee. *(Pretending to be thinking:)* No.

(FRANK *leaves, shutting the door behind him.)*

JACOB: *(Resuming where they left off)* Excuse me, did
I hear—

MARGARET: Yes. I thought I heard a speech coming.
You've written your two books and you've got your
tenure so if you want to have a midlife crisis go on
ahead, because it doesn't matter, does it, you've earned
your right. Well no, I'm sorry. There's another war
going on. If men like you sit on the sidelines, it's lost.
Christ, be alive, that's all. If you had your eyes open
you'd be down in Aaron Goldman's office right now
browbeating that man for behavior that is unacceptable.

JACOB: So that you can go on sleeping with whoever—

MARGARET: Don't reduce it to that.

JACOB: Why not? Isn't that what you're saying? That the
position of men now is to grease the way for women, so

that they can live lives as messy and ridiculous as the ones we've been living for centuries?

MARGARET: That's not what—

JACOB: *(Overlapping on "what")* And suppose even that I were to grant you that it was practicable and—

MARGARET: Right.

JACOB: And *right*. How would I do that, given that I can't even lead a twenty-one year old—a young woman who sat here ten minutes ago—that I can't even find it in me to lead a *child* out of the woods? Tell me, what should I be doing now, running down to Aaron Goldman's office and screaming at him? Would that be rational behavior?

(CHRIS MACADEN, JACOB's office-mate, enters, single-minded as always, goes directly to his desk, deposits a great pile of books, goes right to work. CHRIS is a tall, awkward, gangly man in his mid-thirties, an Ichabod Crane of academia. He walks as if focused on a point directly ahead of him, seeing nothing else.)

JACOB: *(Responding to MARGARET's sudden self-consciousness)* Believe me, he won't hear a word you're saying.

MARGARET: No, I think I've said all I have to say to you.

JACOB: Don't go.

(JACOB follows MARGARET to the door, genuinely eager that she stay with him.)

MARGARET: I'll be late for class. *(Beat. Stops to look at him.)* Yes, as a matter of fact it would be. Rational. Kind. And a step forward, maybe.

(MARGARET exits. JACOB looks around, at the awful emptiness of the room and his life. He looks at CHRIS, then at his own desk, where a huge and pointless pile of papers wait for his attention. He looks again at the door, through

which MARGARET *has just left, as if he might go after her. Then again at* CHRIS, *who is deeply and steadily and even happily at work.)*

JACOB: How do you do it? How do you go on, day after day, marching to your desk, shuffling through your papers, without wanting to blow your brains out?

CHRIS: *(Looks at* JACOB, *no visible response.)* I can't listen to this now. I can't listen to your nihilistic nonsense. *(He goes back to work.)*

JACOB: Why not?

*(*CHRIS *looks at him again. Obviously, something is churning in this guy, because he gets up, opens the door and looks outside, as if to see if anyone is eavesdropping, then comes back in and only then reveals himself.)*

CHRIS: Carole's pregnant.

JACOB: Chris, that's wonderful.

CHRIS: *(As he passes* JACOB, *on the way back to his desk:)* It's personal. No one needs to know. We just found out. He's a little-. He's so small you can't imagine.

JACOB: But my God, this is your first. You should be excited.

CHRIS: He's smaller than the pinpoint of this pencil. There's no guarantee he'll even happen. Meanwhile, there's a hard objective world.

JACOB: Yes. So?

CHRIS: Cling to it, that's all. Even the pronoun. He. Already saddling him with a sex because it's what I want. Why should what I want have anything to do with anything?

JACOB: Nothing. It's how we live, that's all.

CHRIS: Not me. I do not believe in want or hope. I believe in fact. *(As if this is the end of the discussion, he turns back to his desk and resumes work.)*

JACOB: *(Feeling abandoned)* Yes, this is what sends you off to the wilds of Durango, Colorado every summer, to find material for your great critical work.

CHRIS: It may not seem romantic or deep, but it's essential.

JACOB: "Errata in the Works of Zane Grey". Marvelous title.

CHRIS: *(Whipping around in his chair, suddenly confrontational.)* Do you feel proud of your life?

JACOB: *(Taken aback)* Chris.

CHRIS: Do you?

JACOB: I don't know.

CHRIS: Do you wake up in the morning and look at your wife and say—here is a good woman, made better by my presence?

JACOB: No.

CHRIS: Neither do I. I sometimes think if I let myself go entirely, I would probably climb to the top of the Texas School Book Depository and start shooting at whatever moved.

JACOB: Why?

CHRIS: Because I once took a peek inside myself and was frightened to death at what I saw. So I made a choice in life. Close the door to the self. Never for a second look inside. The ancients knew this. We, on the other hand, have leisure time in abundance, so there is a perverse compulsion to do so. I draw the line here. *(With a piece of chalk, he draws a line on the floor between their two desks.)* Your side of the room. Mine. *(Pointing to* JACOB's *"side":)* The realm of the Self. *(Then to his own:)* The realm of logic, clarity, usefulness. *(Again pointing to his own "side":)* Chartres Cathedral. *(Then to* JACOB's:) The Okeefenokee Swamp.

(FRANK *peeks his head back in the door.)*

FRANK: Is she gone?

JACOB: *(Stunned by what* CHRIS *has just said, has to refocus.)* Who? Oh. Yes.

FRANK: *(Stepping in)* Personal stuff?

JACOB: Aaron Goldman dumped her like a hot potato. *(Turning back to* CHRIS:) The Okeefenokee Swamp?

FRANK: Well, she asked for that.

JACOB: Frank.

FRANK: Had it coming, if you ask me.

JACOB: How dare you—

FRANK: Well, the man is married. She knew that very well. He's not very likely to dump Nicole, to leave his sons—

JACOB: That's not the point. You could show a little pity.

FRANK: She's a bloody rock. You could break hammers on her, mark my words. You're merely distracting yourself from a much larger issue. This student you're trying to pawn off on me is properly yours.

JACOB: Why don't you explain Kafka to her, Frank?

FRANK: I wouldn't spend five minutes on the man. This is your area, these modern Europeans, and you are responsible for whatever flirtations you incite in your students.

HOMER: *(From the hall outside)* Hi ho, Hi ho

FRANK: *(Raising his eyes to heaven)* Good God.

(HOMER BOYKIN *enters. He is a diminutive, red-faced man in his sixties, though he perhaps looks older. He has more energy in his frame than the other three men in the room combined.*)

HOMER: Afternoon, lads. Say, here's one you'll like: When the weather's hot and sticky, that's no time to dunk your dickie. When the frost is on the pumpkin, that's the time for dickie dunkin'.

(HOMER *waits for laughter. It isn't forthcoming.*)

JACOB: Where'd you hear that one, Homer?

HOMER: *(Sings)* On the Boardwalk, in Atlantic City.

JACOB: The man knows how to live.

HOMER: *(Rubbing his hands together)* The Trump Taj Mahal. Gamble all day, never see the sun. At night a big lobster, dipped in butter, and then the entertainment. Robert Goulet, Shecky Greene. *(Sings)* If ever I would leave you.

FRANK: We know the song, Homer.

HOMER: I didn't crack a serious book all summer. Spy thrillers. Tom Clancy, that's the ticket.

FRANK: Trust in you, Homer, to put the argument for slumming in the most elegant possible terms. Unfortunately, I'm in a rush. Jacob, this one's yours.

(*He drops* WENDY's *proposal on* JACOB's *desk. As* FRANK *starts out,* HOMER *picks up the proposal.*)

HOMER: "Black Forest". Good Lord, sounds gloomy.

(FRANK *is arrested by this.* HOMER *is his nemesis.*)

HOMER: I wouldn't touch it with a ten foot pole. Haw! Don't know why these students feel they have to come to us with such deadly serious projects. Poor things feel they have to put on the tragic mask or we'll boot them out. One peek into our lives, we could cure them of that misconception, eh, Frank?

FRANK: Yes, well, perhaps.

HOMER: Turn her down, Jacob.

FRANK: *(Hugely bothered by this)* Look, we can't do that.

HOMER: Why not? It's depressing, isn't it? Listen, I turned a student down this morning. Wanted to do poetry. I looked at her stuff, it didn't rhyme.

FRANK: Homer, you know as well as any of us that rhyming's no longer a requirement.

HOMER: Yes, but we earn that freedom, don't we? Don't want them coming in here assuming the legacy of a lot of suicidal poets. Let them get there themselves. Besides, there's a good argument to be made that having to rhyme a poem keeps your head out of the oven. Keeps you at your desk longer, anyway. Turn her down, Jacob. We have the right to what happiness we can get here.

(AARON GOLDMAN enters the office. AARON is an academic cowboy in his late forties. He moves with tremendous confidence. HOMER and FRANK regard him with a respect bordering on awe.)

AARON: This where all the men are gathered? Frank, Homer, good summer?

HOMER: Splendid, Aaron.

FRANK: *(Bowing slightly)* Mister Chairman.

AARON: I'm looking for a tennis partner. Chris, we've never played, have we?

CHRIS: *(As though it's a foreign substance:)* Tennis?

AARON: Yes.

CHRIS: I don't play.

HOMER: I could play with you, Aaron.

AARON: No, sorry. Chris is my man.

CHRIS: What do you do? You hit a ball over a net. What do you do while you're waiting for it to come back?

AARON: You suss out your opponent's moves, try to guess where he's going to hit it.

CHRIS: And what if he misses? You stand there waiting for him to go and get the ball, and self-awareness has a chance to sneak in. You ask, what am I doing? I am a man on a court holding a piece of aluminum and drawn catgut, watching his life eke away—

HOMER: (*Overlapping on "watching"*) God help us when he goes on like this. I was just leaving.

FRANK: As was I.

(FRANK *and* HOMER *exit.* JACOB *is nervous in* AARON's *presence.*)

JACOB: Yes, well, some coffee, I think.

(JACOB *pats his pockets, as if looking for something.* CHRIS *looks suddenly worried.*)

AARON: Jacob, I'd like to have a word with you, when you're back.

JACOB: With me? Fine. Yes.

(JACOB *exits.* CHRIS *and* AARON)

CHRIS: Besides, there are these forty students to place in Freshman Comp sections by five o'clock.

AARON: Oh, we can make quick work of that. You take ten sections, and add four students to each of them.

CHRIS: (*Horrified*) But Aaron, that doesn't take into account their competency, how they placed on exams—

(Very quickly, savagely, AARON *lifts* CHRIS *out of his chair and kisses him hard on the mouth. A long, lingering kiss. When it's finished, and* AARON *lets go,* CHRIS *is quite overpowered, limp, full of self-disgust.)*

AARON: We're going to play a game of tennis, Chris.

CHRIS: Carole's pregnant.

AARON: Ah, good work.

CHRIS: I can't—this—no more.

AARON: We'll talk about that, won't we? Now why don't you go home and put on a pair of shorts and meet me in, say, twenty minutes?

*(*JACOB *comes back with his cup of coffee, just as* CHRIS *starts to exit.)*

JACOB: You're playing, are you?

CHRIS: Well, I suppose it's good for me.

*(*CHRIS *exits.* JACOB *sits at his desk, pretending to be involved in the search for a certain paper.)*

AARON: *(Watching* JACOB *go through his messy piles)* Can I help you with that?

JACOB: No.

AARON: *(Sitting on the edge of* JACOB's *desk)* I wanted to talk to you about—no doubt Margaret's already told you—I couldn't help noticing her coming out of your door a while ago. I don't think I handled the breakup very well.

*(*JACOB *sips his coffee, not wanting to answer.)*

AARON: I just hope you're not caught in a bind, having to choose between us. I would hate to see it affect our friendship, is all.

JACOB: *(Nodding his head, avoiding engagement)* No. No, of course not.

AARON: *(Sure of* JACOB *now)* There were issues—
we won't discuss them here, but—trust that whatever
she tells you, there was more to it. *(Beat)* Well. *(On his
way to the door:)* Glad about this.

JACOB: *(As much a surprise to him as to* AARON:*)* She
wanted me to—well, she went on a bit about civility—
you know, her hobby horse. *(He's being too nice about
this, against his better instincts.)* She seemed to think
I should chew you out, that I should stand up for—
something, I can't remember—

AARON: *(Amused, as he assumes he's intended to be)* Yes.
I can imagine how all that would appeal to you, the
Bard of Futility.

*(*JACOB *is deflated by this.)*

AARON: Well, 'ta.

*(*AARON *exits.* JACOB *looks after him, alone with the subtle
condemnation* AARON *has left behind. Then he lifts a piece
of paper off his desk, stares at it, picks up the phone, dials.)*

JACOB: Hello, is Wendy there? Her roommate. Well,
would you tell her when she comes in that Professor
Freundlich called. She was just in my office, asking me
to work with her on an Independent. Would you tell
her— *(Hesitates a moment.)* Tell her yes. *(Surprised.
Scared. He hangs up.)*

(Immediately, Robert Goulet's version of If Ever I Would
Leave You *[the autumn verse] starts up, as the lights
cross-fade to:)*

Scene Two

*(*MARGARET'*s house)*

(It is mid-Fall now, about six weeks after Scene One. Outside
MARGARET'*s house, a tree with yellow leaves falling. A front*
porch extends from the house. A baby swing hangs from the
branch of a tree, a child's toys scattered on the porch.)

*(*MARGARET *sits on the porch, absorbed in her work: open*
texts, a legal pad she is writing on.)

*(*JACOB *is passing by, carrying a briefcase full of books and*
papers, on his way home. He stops, looks up at the house,
then carries on. He stops again, as if amazed by his own
momentary ability to break out of the mold of habit.
He starts toward the porch, uncertain as to whether he
has the right to disturb her.)

JACOB: *(Quietly)* Margaret?

MARGARET: *(Pleased to see him)* Oh. Did you stop by for
a visit?

JACOB: *(His customary excuse for himself)* I was just—

MARGARET: Please say yes. I'm desperate to get a break
from this. *(Getting up, excited)* I'll get us a drink.

JACOB: I don't have to—

MARGARET: *(She's already inside)* I've only got wine.
Red or white? Oops. I've only got red.

JACOB: *(As if he has to decide)* I'll take red.

MARGARET: *(Coming outside with the wine)* Sara's
napping. I must look a mess.

JACOB: *(Still resisting the invitation)* No. No! This is your
work time?

MARGARET: Relax. Please. Sit down. For a minute.
Come *on.*

(JACOB *gives in, accepts the wine, then looks around,
feeling the atmosphere of her yard. It's nice.*)

JACOB: Why do I feel this is such a huge transgression
for me?

MARGARET: *(Sitting, relaxing)* Yes. Why?

JACOB: I am—due home. My wife expects me. A certain
time. She knows I've left the office.

MARGARET: And?

JACOB: Well, there's a certain rigor to domestic life.
Duties. Errands. Obligations. If you don't keep it up,
le deluge. A maze of expectation. *(Beat. Wanting to change
the subject)* How's your healing?

MARGARET: What? *Oh.* I'm all right. No thanks to you.
No man on the horizon at present. Probably good for
me. It's all right. Achingly lonely. But all right. *(Beat)*
You wouldn't know anything about that, of course.
A warm bed every night. There's the reward for your
maze of expectation. A companion.

JACOB: Yes. Except that lately it seems we might as
well be sleeping on separate moons. Revolving around
the sun of our children, our—life. She gets tired.
I shouldn't—really—It's disloyal.

MARGARET: *(Beat. Looking at him, studying him.)* Have
you ever—I've always wanted to ask you—ever—

JACOB: Been unfaithful?

MARGARET: Yes.

JACOB: No.

MARGARET: Twenty years?

JACOB: Eighteen. No. Never. Once. A kiss. A long time ago. A kiss. Once.

MARGARET: A student?

JACOB: No. A colleague. Female, let me hasten to add. In graduate school. In the library stacks. Near a volume—I'll never forget this—called "Mending Books is Fun". Seventeen years ago..

MARGARET: And since then?

JACOB: Nothing.

MARGARET: Ever miss it?

JACOB: *Please.* It's all I can do right now to walk this path. Office to home. Home to classroom. Praying that when I address my class the right words come out of my mouth. Hoping I'm on the right subject. Someday, I expect to find them all staring at me, their pencils dropped, mouths agape— "no no no, this isn't *Joyce*, Professor." *(Beat)* It astounds me that I once thought, in the bloom of youth, that this was something— well, that anything, I suppose, was something—that could sustain a man. *(Beat. Regarding her)* Comment?

MARGARET: No. I'm just listening.

JACOB: The *hell.* I can imagine what you're thinking. Tonight, you know what I'm supposed to do? Play soccer with my son. He's thirteen—well, you've met him, he's awkward. But determined, for some reason— peer pressure—he wants to be good. I assistant coach the team. So tonight, a little extra practice. I'll stand there—I can see this as if it's already happened, but then, that's the way I feel about three fourths of my life—I'll be shouting something or other—"Good! Yes! Good!" But it wouldn't surprise me to hear myself saying, "No, *fuck* soccer, you don't have to be *good* at this. Rip something more *basic* out of life than *achievement.*"

MARGARET: *(Beat)* Perhaps that would be good advice.

JACOB: *(Called back to himself.)* Would it? I don't know.
Well. *(Puts his glass down, checks his watch)* I should go.
It's been delightful.

MARGARET: What's that basic thing you want to rip out
of life?

*(*JACOB *smiles at* MARGARET, *aware that she's consciously
drawing him out.)*

JACOB: I don't *like* being in this state. I don't *like* feeling
like I've fallen off the edge of the world. So part of me
thinks, I should just be patient, *wait.* And another part,
something you said—

MARGARET: *(Intrigued)* Oh. What?

JACOB: No. I shouldn't give you this ammunition.

MARGARET: Oh come on.

JACOB: Well. Well. That I'm wasting time. Living on
excuses. Yes. We should be pushing things forward.
Here we are. This is the academy. There ought to be
some action for me to perform. *(In the course of his last
few speeches, he's picked up his wine, a nervous gesture as
much as anything. Now he puts it down.)* I'm sorry. I just
go on sometimes.

MARGARET: And now *I'm* sorry. I hear Sara crying.
I have to go in. *(She gets up.)* But I want to hear more
of this.

JACOB: No. I'll just—

MARGARET: *(Urgent)* Please. Stay a minute. Call your
wife, or something. Really.

JACOB: *(When she's at the door, ready to go in)* I'm not that
interesting. You're just lonely.

MARGARET: *(A moment. Admitting that he's hit on a truth)*
I am. Yes. But—stay.

(MARGARET *looks at* JACOB, *then goes in. He is drawn, almost immediately, to her notes, which she has left scattered on the porch. As soon as he begins reading, a natural cynicism starts up in him, something combative to offset the vulnerability he's recently displayed. Then he hears her returning and puts them down.*)

MARGARET: Thank God. She went back. Little cries. Hell doing it alone, really. Have to be everything. Where were we?

JACOB: I've been reading your notes.

MARGARET: You don't have to sneak looks.

JACOB: What an odd project for a feminist scholar. Maid Marian.

MARGARET: *(A little more testy than the remark warrants)* Please don't call her that.

JACOB: *(Taking a step back, but only for a second)* Marian. Right. What's next for you, the Fairy Godmother?

MARGARET: We were talking about something else, I think.

JACOB: But really, what *is* this about?

MARGARET: Oh, this is so typical. You're actually *revealing* something of yourself. So here, let's distract ourselves. But all right, I'd be happy to explain. There have been points in time where things have been utterly topsy turvy, unallowable as history. We cannot have strong women unless they're sexually safe. So Marion's been turned into the simpering maid, the faithful virgin wearing a ridiculous hat, waiting for Robin while he went off and had fun. The record—at least, the record of ballad, of myth—suggests something different.

JACOB: Yes?

MARGARET: She was in control. She ruled him. He used to dance for her.

JACOB: *(Beat)* Yes?

MARGARET: *For* her. *He* was the sex object. He let himself be looked at.

JACOB: Really? Robin Hood did that?

MARGARET: *(Beat. Taking in his subtle mocking of her, tacitly allowing it.)* According to—Adam de la Halle, yes. And here's the trick, which is sort of wonderful. He could do that—allow himself to be the sex object, the woman, if you will—because he thought so very highly of himself.

(JACOB is thoughtful.)

MARGARET: And your reaction would be?

JACOB: I envision a best seller.

(MARGARET smiles)

JACOB: A vehicle for Tom and Nicole. We're seeing the last of you.

MARGARET: But putting ourselves in this situation— for a moment, for *fun*—the point is interesting, isn't it? A man can do nothing without a certain self esteem.

(JACOB listens, skeptically.)

MARGARET: Believing that being dull and dutiful, that walking the path, without conviction, can support young lives, never mind *older* ones—that idea would have been thrown out with the slops in Marian's time. We're getting it *all* wrong. Men are supposed to be men. It's just that they need to figure out how to do that while—elevating women.

JACOB: Yes. Neat trick.

(Beat. A moment between them)

MARGARET: But, well, look at you. Walking this path everyday as if each deviation represents an unthinkable

transgression of the rules—even the way you conduct
your marriage

JACOB: Please don't start this.

MARGARET: Sorry. Just doesn't seem fair. I'm looking
for a little intellectual companionship, a little sharing of
souls, a glass of *wine*, for Christ's sake, you've got to—
what? Go home and vacuum? Practice soccer? Does
your son not have friends? Does he not have a private
life? Thirteen? Time to masturbate? Are you scheduling
that in for him? *(Beat. Aware of herself)* Sorry. It's
loneliness. Go home. *(She begins picking up after herself.)*

JACOB: Let me help you.

MARGARET: No. I'm fine.

JACOB: Margaret, please. I'm an innocent victim here.
I stopped for a moment. I knew I shouldn't have.

MARGARET: *Why? Why?* Why is it impossible that two
people, just because one is married, can't share *more*?

JACOB: I don't know.

*(JACOB hands MARGARET her notes. A look passes between
them.)*

MARGARET: Sara will be up soon.

JACOB: Yes.

MARGARET: *(Beat)* It's what's charming about you,
really. Anyone else, given the hints I've dropped here,
would have been on top of me in about ten seconds.

JACOB: *(Still somehow incredulous)* Is all of this an
invitation?

MARGARET: Maybe. Don't know. Don't know that you
could handle it, really. A man whose entire extramarital
experience seems to have been a kiss in the library
stacks, during which you were apparently detached

enough to notice what book you were pressing her against.

(JACOB *is silent a moment.*)

JACOB: I don't know how to accept this. You flatter me. *(Beat)* I keep thinking there's someone behind me you're talking to. This is—*me*, correct?

MARGARET: Correct. Yes. But I'm losing nerve by the moment.

(JACOB *stares at* MARGARET, *at first paralyzed, then moves toward her, takes her hand. A moment later, kisses her)*

MARGARET: We won't have time for anything today—

JACOB: No—

(Beat. The next two lines said simultaneously.)

JACOB: My—

MARGARET: She'll—

(Beat. JACOB *draws* MARGARET *to him.)*

JACOB: *(Holding her, stroking the back of her head with great tenderness)* Ah me.

(Lights fade, as Mitch Miller's version of We Need a Little Christmas *comes up. Lights rise on:)*

Scene Three

(A Christmas party at the LEECH's*)*

(Holly festooned around doorways, and above. A woman on a couch, HEIDI LEECH, *looking very drunk and at the same time entirely composed. She is petite, grau-haired, primly dressed. Thirty years of marriage to* FRANK *have rubbed some of his Englishness off on her, but she is a child of Maine.* FRANK *is on the opposite end of the couch from her, smoking a cigar. Next to the couch,* JACOB *sits in an armchair. In a corner of the room, at a remove from the others,* JACOB's *wife,* LEAH, *sits, her nose buried in a coffee table art book, flipping the pages, detached from the scene. She is long-legged, long haired, aloof, pretty in a slightly past-it way, a woman who no longer devotes an enormous amount of energy to how she appears.)*

(On the walls, there are bookcases full of books. The room looks festive. Sound of others, from an adjoining room.)

HEIDI: *(Singing, with stars in her eyes)*
It was fascination, I know
It was fascination the moment I found you
Fascination da da dum da da dum...

JACOB: Drunk again, eh, Heidi?

HEIDI: Nostalgic. *(She goes on humming the tune, in her own world.)*

FRANK: It's those damn V C Rs, if you ask me. She goes out and rents these romantic pictures, hell on a marriage.

HEIDI: *Love in the Afternoon,* 1957. Gary Cooper, Audrey Hepburn. *(With special appreciation for the sound of the words:)* Maurice Chevalier. *(Goes on humming)*

FRANK: For years, woman had to make do with what was on television. Farrah Fawcett-Majors in *How I Burned My Husband to Death in Bed* —do you remember that one? Domestic life seemed a goddamned Eden in comparison. Now they have recourse to all this romantic slop.

HEIDI: When I saw *Love is a Many-Splendored Thing* was on video, I wanted to *steal* the bloody thing. We had no children then. Frank would take me to the Loew's Orpheum in Boston and put his hand under my skirt.

(LEAH *looks up for the first time.*)

FRANK: Oh, good God.

HEIDI: He was in Graduate School then. It seemed—tell me if this is true—you would walk down a street, a row of theatres, and every movie would be somehow about *your* life, *your* dreams. Deborah Kerr in *Count Your Blessings.* How to survive your husband's infidelities, an important thing to learn. And they were all done with wit and charm. Doesn't it seem that in every one of those movies, somewhere along the line Maurice Chevalier would make an appearance, offering a bit of Gallic wisdom? *(She pours more wine into her glass.)* The lifted eyebrow, the raunchy half-laugh. *(She sighs happily.)* And you felt your problems were manageable. Well, you walk down the same street today, there are none of those wonderful old theatres. All gone. Replaced by junk shops frequented by— *(Distinctly pronouncing all three syllables:)* Puerto Rican women. All the movies are out at the wretched malls. It's the Age of the Roman numeral. Cinema I, II, III, IV, featuring this one II, the other one III. Starring people I've never heard of, doing things I wouldn't dream of watching. Black men who talk fast. Women wearing sexy skirts. *(She hoists her own skirt up, does an impression of a Latin sexpot.)* "Chinga chinga chinga"

FRANK: *(Long-suffering)* Heidi.

HEIDI: And who goes to those movies, anyway?
Whose dreams do they express? When they explore
our times someday, they'll say we went from an age
of gold and iron to an age of junk. Junk stores, junk
movies, junk people. A big dumb country without
the balls to maintain an elite. Perhaps we ought to
call this America II. It's certainly not the original.

FRANK: Yes, thank you, Heidi, for the Federalist view
of contemporary culture, but don't you find it the
slightest bit queer that though we're the hosts of this
party, all the guests seem to be in the other room?

JACOB: What about us?

HEIDI: Jacob and Leah. You'll always listen to me,
won't you?

(JACOB *and* LEAH *look at each other, amused by* HEIDI
*without necessarily agreeing with anything she says.
They should seem, at this moment, very much a couple,
of one mind.*)

HEIDI: Anyway, I don't care if we are the hosts. This is
not Christmas. This is not Christmas like I remember it.

JACOB: Are we about to be treated to a memoir of the
glorious Christmases in old Maine?

(FRANK *shakes his head and smiles.*)

HEIDI: Good heavens, no. That was all poverty and
grimness and dread. No, for me Christmas will always
be associated with cities. Places where people come
together, rub up against one another the way they used
to, in the early sixties, before it all fell apart. Remember?
Jack and Jackie were in the White House and, well,
didn't it seem we all took care of one another then?
Didn't you feel that way, Jacob?

JACOB: I was five.

HEIDI: Yes, but didn't your parents feel that way? Oh, I'm sure they did. Everyone did. It was our flowering, the nation's best moment. I was pregnant with Benjamin, remember, Frank?

(CHRIS *comes hurtling into the room, pours himself a drink, very serious.*)

CHRIS: She's upstairs throwing up.

HEIDI: *(Sympathetic)* Oh, Chris.

CHRIS: She's been throwing up for three months straight. When does it stop?

HEIDI: *(Leading him to the sofa, sitting him down beside her)* Dear boy, let me take your head in my arms. There, there. Soon it will all stop and you'll have a fine son or daughter. Not that it will matter one bit, because who in their right mind would want to be born into this Age of Junk?

FRANK: Now Heidi, there's no need for that.

CHRIS: Will he be born, that's my question. *(Bangs his head with his fist, reproving himself)* He. She. It. Whatever.

HEIDI: Oh, he'll be born all right. Babies do survive their mother's nausea. But really, think of what this child will never be exposed to. Phil Silvers. Jimmy Durante. Eddie Lawrence. Jack Benny. *(Getting up)* Oh, I'd abort it if I were you.

CHRIS: *(Horrified)* Good God.

(MARGARET *enters, from the direction where the party noises have been heard.*)

MARGARET: May I join you?

(JACOB *stands on her entrance, with a kind of juiced-up awareness.* LEAH *notices this.*)

HEIDI: Oh, please do. That is, if you don't mind listening to my diatribe against our rotten age.

FRANK: Yes, remember life on the old plantation, Heidi?

HEIDI: Oh, stop. *(To* MARGARET, *but not quietly or discreetly:)* Now listen, dear, I've mentioned to Nicole Goldman that she's not to say anything embarrassing to you about your affair with her husband.

MARGARET: *(Beat. Taken aback)* Thank you, I'd have preferred for you to have said that to me in private.

HEIDI: What does it matter? We all know what happened. There are no secrets here. The whole point is to avoid public embarrassment.

MARGARET: *(Looking at the others)* Yes, thank you, Heidi. *(Focusing on* LEAH, *who is immersed in her book)* Hello, Leah.

(LEAH *looks up, smiles wanly.)*

HEIDI: *(Moving purposefully to the stereo)* Now that we have a quorum, I'm going to play some of the music I've been saving up.

FRANK: No more Mitch Miller, please.

HEIDI: No. Perish the thought. *(Listing the needle, suddenly animated, introducing a game)* What are your favorite Christmas scenes from the movies?

MARGARET: *It's a Wonderful Life.*

HEIDI: Oh, don't be so typical, dear. Favorite Christmas scenes from movies a little less over*exposed* than *It's a Wonderful Life.*

JACOB: *The F B I Story.*

FRANK: *(Chuckling)* Jacob.

JACOB: *(Defending his perfectly defensible choice)* Oh, it broke your heart. When Jimmy Stewart had to leave his family on Christmas Eve to go and capture Killer McCall.

HEIDI: That is a good one, but I don't have the music, unfortunately. Now here's one. *(Lifts the needle, ready to play)* Christmas Eve in New York City. A lonely bachelor—

JACOB: *Bell, Book & Candle!*

(JACOB's clearly showing off for MARGARET now, and LEAH picks up on this.)

HEIDI: No.

JACOB: A great one!

HEIDI: Yes. But no. A lonely bachelor—

LEAH: *(The sense that she's saying this—entering the game—only because she's aware of what's going on between JACOB and MARGARET)* The Apartment.

HEIDI: *(Glee)* Yes!

JACOB: You don't know movies. I'm supposed to get this.

(LEAH looks at him with a certain competitive pride, goes back to her book.)

HEIDI: Now imagine yourself sitting in the plush deep chairs of the Loew's Orpheum in Boston in 1960.

FRANK: *(Anticipating her)* Jack and Jackie in the White House. Lynchings in Mississippi.

HEIDI: *(In a reverie)* Outside, you can hear the gentle tinkling of the Salvation Army Santa ringing his bells. The credits begin to roll.

JACOB: Frank sneaks his hand up your dress.

HEIDI: Ladies and gentleman, the double pianos of Ferrante and Teicher play the Theme from *The Apartment.*

(HEIDI lowers the needle. The record plays. She is in ecstasy. The others, not knowing what else to do, sit and seriously

listen. But as the music goes on, and as they realize they're trapped listening to it, looks of boredom and confusion begin to appear on their faces.)

JACOB: *(To save them all:)* Remember the Christmas scene from *Spartacus*?

HEIDI: *(Still in her revery)* Yes. *(Then, sudden recognition:)* Oh, Jacob, there was no Christmas scene in *Spartacus*.

JACOB: Yes, but only because Kubrick was so cold. Spielberg would have worked one in.

CHRIS: *(Trying to effect an escape)* I think I'll go and see if she's all right.

HEIDI: Bring her some ginger ale, Chris.

JACOB: *(Same idea of escape)* Yes. I'll help.

HEIDI: . *(Taking* JACOB's *hand, to keep him there)* And you'll stay here, Jacob. This is only the beginning to the little medley I have prepared.

(CHRIS *exits upstairs just as* NICOLE GOLDMAN *enters, coming from the direction of the party. She is a heavy, buxom woman, quite attractive, used to taking over by her presence, any room she enters. Very savvy, misses nothing)*

NICOLE: *(Husky French accent)* Is this where the interesting things are being said? I can tell you, it's the Sahara desert in there.

HEIDI: Oh, I'm so glad you're joining us, Nicole. You know Margaret Olin, don't you? Nicole *Goldman.*

MARGARET: *(Chagrined)* Yes.

HEIDI: *Aaron's* wife.

MARGARET: *(Excruciating)* Yes. Hello.

HEIDI: Aren't we civilized? Isn't this wonderful? I almost feel as though Maurice Chevalier himself had entered the room.

NICOLE: *(Moving to plop herself down on the couch next to FRANK)* Will you shut up with your terrible ideas about the French? How are you, Jacob?

JACOB: I'm fine, Nicole.

NICOLE: Leah, we hardly see you.

(LEAH turns a page, looks up. She smiles, barely, then goes back to the book.)

JACOB: *(His annoyance at her finally surfacing)* Leah. *(To NICOLE:)* Excuse her. She gets bored easily at these parties.

LEAH: *(Not giving an inch)* Don't make excuses for me, please. I don't get bored at all.

NICOLE: Heidi, there is more food? I'm starved.

HEIDI: The chicken wasn't filling for you?

NICOLE: You have forty people and you served enough for four.

HEIDI: Well, I hoped they wouldn't stay long.

NICOLE: Why have a Christmas party and starve people?

HEIDI: It was Frank's idea, really.

FRANK: Confound it, Heidi, you blame this one on me every year, but you know damn well it's always your idea.

NICOLE: Where is Homer this year? I haven't seen him.

(NICOLE looks around for an answer. An awkward silence)

HEIDI: Aaron hasn't told you?

NICOLE: He tells me nothing.

FRANK: An unfortunate incident.

NICOLE: He's all right?

HEIDI: He put his hand on a student's knee.

FRANK: Oh, Heidi, he did more than that and you know it.

HEIDI: And uttered certain blasphemies.

FRANK: *(Calmly correcting the historical record)* He came unstuck, apparently, during a conference.

HEIDI: Down on his knees and howling like a dog.

FRANK: Heidi!

HEIDI: Oh, Nicole will forgive him.

NICOLE: What did he do to her?

(Silence)

FRANK: *(Clearing his throat)* He bit her on the knee, apparently.

JACOB: Wait. Do we know that? It seems like— everybody's jumping to conclusions.

HEIDI: *(Line overlaps with* JACOB'S *"everybody's")* I can't find it in myself to do anything but forgive the poor man. Fortunately, Frank is on the committee that will decide Homer's fate.

NICOLE: He should be booted out. Don't you agree with me, Margaret? *(Giving her only a second to respond)* It's a wonder professors ever get any teaching done—the atmosphere is so, how you say?

JACOB: *(Good natured ribbing of a woman he enjoys)* You've been here twenty years. What is this, "how you say"? And how can you say, right off the bat, he should be booted out? This is someone we like.

FRANK: Perhaps we should cut this discussion short. *(Shifting in his chair. He loves the feeling of power)* I don't think the President, were she to know, would look kindly on my participating in an open discussion like this.

(CHRIS *enters.*)

CHRIS: She's lying on your bed. I hope that's all right.

HEIDI: *(A little worried)* She's finished throwing up, then?

CHRIS: Yes.

NICOLE: *(Looking him over)* Throwing up, your wife? You are still making love to her, Chris?

CHRIS: *(On his guard)* Why do you ask that?

NICOLE: *(Testing him)* It's possible she's looking for attention, that's all.

CHRIS: She gets plenty of attention.

NICOLE: Chris would never bite a student's knee.

CHRIS: No. I never would.

(NICOLE *gives him a moment's further scrutiny, then looks around the room.*)

NICOLE: This still does not explain. The student whose knee was bitten, she is not here?

HEIDI: No. We didn't invite her.

NICOLE: So why is Homer not here?

HEIDI: Well, I suppose because he wasn't invited.

FRANK: *(A masterful performance)* Did we leave him off the list?

HEIDI: *(Trying to save herself)* Yes. Well. I'd assumed— something or other. I can't imagine what. Assumed he shouldn't be invited, I suppose. *(A desperate attempt to brighten things:)* I'll get the cake. Shall I?

NICOLE: Oh. Please. What kind is it?

HEIDI: *(On her way out:)* Black Forest.

JACOB: Frank, it's all lovely we're keeping our mouths shut, but shouldn't we at least *talk* about Homer?

FRANK: *(Beat. An awkward moment.)* How are your sons, Nicole?

NICOLE: Big. Enormous. Giants. Who is their father, I wonder. Who is their mother? Chris, whatever you get, I guarantee you will not recognize. That is the only guarantee.

JACOB: Oh, I don't know. I recognize my children pretty well. Maybe too well.

LEAH: *(Alerted)* What's that mean?

JACOB: Nothing. *(To her continued, critical stare:)* Nothing.

LEAH: Is that a complaint?

JACOB: *(Defensive)* No. I guess I'd like to be more surprised sometimes, that's all.

FRANK: *(Appreciatively; maybe even a little silly in his envy)* Still stars of the gridiron, are they, Nicole, your sons?

NICOLE: Savages. Big black eyes. They sleep like bears in their beds. What is that play, you would know this, Frank, where the princes go into a cave?

FRANK: That would be *Cymbeline*.

NICOLE: Yes. We saw it in London. Two princes in a cave. Sons of a professor and a—well, I am not much but at least I read. And what do I get as my reward for being civilized? Burps and farts.

HEIDI: *(Entering with a very small cake, on a tray with plates.)* Here it is.

(HEIDI displays it on the table, with pride. The rest simply stare at it.)

NICOLE: For forty people, Heidi?

HEIDI: Well. Yes.

NICOLE: My God, you put out six dried-out chicken wings and a rind of cheese I'd be embarrassed to throw to the birds, and this is supposed to make up for it?

HEIDI: *(Slicing the cake, quite proud of herself)* It's very hard to make, you know. There's an endless amount of folding and whipping and separating of eggs. Let's see, how many of us are there?

FRANK: What about the others?

HEIDI: Let them rot.

(HEIDI hands out plates of cake.)

NICOLE: What is this I smell, kirsch?

HEIDI: Yes. Cherry kirsch. It's where the cake gets its name. It's an old Viennese recipe, but cherry kirsch is made in the Black Forest.

NICOLE: *(Tasting hers)* This is magnificent. The cherry kirsch, my God.

HEIDI: Yes, the Germans got at least one thing right.

JACOB: That's a phrase you hear all the time. Black Forest. But does anyone know where it is?

CHRIS: I've been there.

LEAH: *(Not looking up)* So have I.

JACOB: *(Curious, surprised)* Have you?

HEIDI: Someone should get the atlas. Frank, where is it?

FRANK: Should be in the bookcase. Jacob is closest. Up there, Jacob. The tall red one.

HEIDI: Oh, what fun. We'll look it up.

(HEIDI receives the book from JACOB.)

CHRIS: It's in Germany.

HEIDI: Well, we *know* that, Chris. *(Consulting the index)* England, Scotland, France, Germany—here it is. It should be this green area over here. *(Following the map with her finger)* But no. Isn't that queer. It's this brown area.

CHRIS: It's very hard to find, actually.

HEIDI: *(Reading the map)* Freudenstadt. Schramberg. Rottweil. Anyone who goes to Germany must be mad. Imagine pulling into Rottweil and saying your name is Cohn. They probably gas you on sight.

CHRIS: I was there. Junior year abroad. At Tubingen. Went backpacking. With a girl. We went to the Black Forest.

HEIDI: *(Obsessed with the map, she might as well be alone in the room.)* Freiberg-im-Breisgau. Dreadful.

FRANK: I think Chris is trying to tell us a story.

HEIDI: Oh, are you, Chris? I'm sorry.

CHRIS: It's nothing. It's not a story. I was at Tubingen and there was a girl. That's all.

NICOLE: Did you sleep with her?

CHRIS: Why are you embarrassing me with all these sex questions?

NICOLE: Because you fascinate me.

CHRIS: *(Beat)* Well yes I slept with her.

HEIDI: In the Black Forest.

(CHRIS is locked into his memory, unaware that HEIDI and NICOLE, to a lesser degree, the others, are now hanging on his every word. Finally he looks up and becomes aware of them.)

CHRIS: What do you all want to know?

HEIDI: What *happened*?

CHRIS: We took this backpacking trip. We were sleeping outdoors, under the stars. Someone came. It was near this old hotel, this hotel that was like a hotel in a dream. Someone came and she left me.

NICOLE: Another man?

CHRIS: Yes.

HEIDI: *(As if the word is synonymous with "villain")* A German.

CHRIS: Yes. I think so.

HEIDI: Oh, tell us more.

CHRIS: *(He looks around at the company, then at his dish of cake.)* We'd all been together—the three of us, this one night. Eating. And then he told stories. I didn't like him. You know these people you meet when you're traveling. Loose nuts rolling around the world, not clamped down anywhere, they're dangerous. But I...well you know how it is when you are young and you are out of your accustomed place. *(He burrows back in.)*

HEIDI: You what?

CHRIS: Nothing, nothing happened, really. When I woke up in the morning, they were both gone and I went somewhere to get coffee, this old hotel. I asked the proprietor, where is the Black Forest. He said you're in it. *(He finishes his cake. Very solemn)*

NICOLE: Surely you must have done something to make her leave you.

CHRIS: *(Uncomfortable)* No. Nothing.

NICOLE: You don't remember it, or you've crossed it out.

CHRIS: That's not the point I'm making here.

FRANK: *(Saving him)* He's talking about the inexplicability of things. I think.

CHRIS: Yes. That's it. Where did he come from—that man. And why did he have to show up on that night? And now this baby. Is he a dream, too? Does he grow up and do well? Does he fall into a pool? Does the house go up in flames in our sleep? Do I get a shotgun some night and kill us all? How do you know?

HEIDI: *(Consoling)* Oh, Chris.

NICOLE: The girl. Did you see her again?

CHRIS: Yes. Back in Tubingen. We never spoke. It was like she had erased me. And I let it happen. I didn't fight.

JACOB: A chilling story.

HEIDI: *(Wistful, but returning to the hostess mode)* The coffee should be ready, I think.

(She exits. An uncomfortable silence in the room)

CHRIS: I'm sorry for spoiling everyone's mood.

JACOB: Oh, we were in splendid moods, Chris. *(Picking up a record)* Heidi was about to play the theme from *Holiday for Lovers* by the Norman Luboff Choir.

CHRIS: It's just—I wanted to make a point, I suppose. Perhaps it's not a point to be made at a party, but my wife has gotten me all upset.

JACOB: *(Getting excited)* Oh, I like your point. The fact is, if it were an event in a novel, a twentieth century novel, a twentieth century *European* novel, that man who came and stole away your girlfriend—the dream logic would be perfect because you'd hunt him down and eventually you'd realize he was a manifestation of yourself.

NICOLE: I hate those novels.

JACOB: We all do. Do you realize I have spent my life devoted to books like those and I don't believe in them anymore.

(LEAH *looks up, intrigued now.*)

JACOB: *(The next line or two are directed to* CHRIS.*)*
The fact is, there is a reason why she left you. It's not all about "the unexplainable". We do things. They lead to other things. People see things in us that for years we thought we were hiding. Things end. Where are those novels? Where is the cause and effect school of literature? I am a man who has spent twenty years torturing students.

MARGARET: You haven't been torturing students.

JACOB: *(A speech he means sincerely, and like a man not used to speaking sincerely, he may go a bit overboard in the realm of passion.)* No, I have. Because I don't think it's true anymore. The *grand mal* of the twentieth century, two world wars, the Holocaust, the Bomb, alienated Man—hello, the sun came out . It stopped raining.

FRANK: We are in the presence now of the Ronald Reagan School of Literary Theory.

JACOB: Yes, make fun, okay, but tell me, does anyone seriously believe that Franz Kafka has his finger on the pulse? Is that our lives? My students leave class, they want—ordinary things. Love. Connection. And they might get it. They're making progress, do you know that? They're *closer* to being able to understand each other than we ever were. And what do I teach them? *The Castle. The Good Soldier Schweik.* They think I'm a joke.

MARGARET: *(Made uncomfortable by where he's going)*
I think Heidi might need some help.

JACOB: Don't go. It's coffee. (*As if the concept of "help"
as* MARGARET *meant it is suddenly inexplicable to him.*)
Coffee. That's all.

(*The last moment between them has been too revealingly
tender.* LEAH *is not the only one to notice.*)

NICOLE: I wish I could believe what you are saying.
I take one look at my sons and the text that comes to
mind is *The Hairy Ape.* I look at them eating breakfast
and I believe we have made no progress since we began
standing on two legs. Worse. That we are going
backwards.

JACOB: No, but look at Chris' story—

HEIDI: (*Entering with a flourish. Tray with coffee things.*)
Here we are. (*Laying out the service*) Everyone. Cream
and sugar.

MARGARET: (*Relieved that* JACOB *has been interrupted*)
Thank God. Jacob has been lecturing us.

JACOB: (*Willing to see it as a joke*) All right, so I'll shut up.
But I'm saying something. We all listen to Chris' story,
we genuflect by rote at the altar of unknowability,
but I'll bet you did something, you dog.

(AARON *enters. His presence immediately makes* JACOB,
MARGARET *and* CHRIS *a little nervous.*)

AARON: Do I smell coffee?

HEIDI: (*Welcoming*) Aaron, come in.

AARON: Trying to keep it from the rest of us?

HEIDI: Was it you who was making everyone laugh so?
I bet it was. Oh, make me laugh. You used to do that
for me.

(HEIDI *hands* AARON *a cup of coffee.*)

AARON: I can't do it on cue. (*Noticing that they've been
eating*) Was this a cake?

HEIDI: Yes. Everyone was ravenous. We cleaned it up, I'm afraid.

AARON: None left, then?

HEIDI: Afraid not.

AARON: No one wants to share any of what's left on his plate?

(Beat. No one offers. In fact, they all rush to finish what's on their plates before he can get to it.)

HEIDI: Are you hungry, Aaron?

AARON: No. No, Heidi. The chicken wing was just fine.

JACOB: I want a cigar. Frank, do you mind?

FRANK: Help yourself.

(JACOB takes a cigar out of FRANK's humidor puts it in his mouth.)

FRANK: You have to cut it, Jacob. You'll find the cutter by the humidor.

JACOB: *(Finds the cutter, but is at a loss how to use it)* Ah.

AARON: *(Stepping forward to demonstrate how to cut a cigar)* Like this, Jacob.

FRANK: *(Pointing)* And the matches.

JACOB: *(Taken slightly aback by the embarrassment of having to have all this shown to him, particularly in front of MARGARET)* Where are these from?

FRANK: Honduras, Jacob.

JACOB: *(Finally having the cigar lit, kicking back a little)* Why don't I have habits like this? By God, this is enjoyable.

(They all look at him: JACOB's pose is uncharacteristic, and thus, fairly ridiculous.)

AARON: Perhaps there's a reason, Jacob.

JACOB: What, do I look silly? I don't care if I do.

AARON: It must mean the party's winding down if we're drinking coffee. Got to be up early tomorrow morning for a Search Committee meeting.

NICOLE: Oh, let them enjoy themselves. Always shooing everyone out once you've had your good time.

AARON: It won't wait, I'm afraid. We're hiring someone for the Ethnic Studies position.

HEIDI: Will it have to be a black, Aaron?

AARON: *(Awkward, looking at the others)* I think it's likely to be, given the pool of applicants.

HEIDI: Oh, dear. That will stiffen things up in the Department, won't it?

FRANK: Heidi, please.

HEIDI: *(Bulling on ahead)* Oh, look, I'm as liberal as anyone else, Frank, but it's— *(She goes to the doorway leading to the other guests, to make sure the coast is clear. Her speech should continue uninterrupted.)* —impossible to *talk* to black people these days and you know it as well as I do. Ten, twenty, even thirty years ago it was much easier. I'm lost—someone tell me what word I'm supposed to use these days? Black? African American? Person of color? Never mind what it is I'm supposed to believe these days about race. I don't even know. We couldn't be *having* this conversation right now if there were a black person in the room.

AARON: That may be so, but it would be hard to justify one of us teaching the Black Literature course.

HEIDI: *(Plowing ahead)* Oh. Look: is it really necessary to have an entire course devoted to black writing? None of it is that *good*. Am I saying something shocking? I've tried to read those writers, and

well—Toni Morrison with her ghosts, and the other
one—the lesbian letter writer—

*(They are all sitting—or standing—there, as if afraid to
move. HEIDI's speech ought to seem as much to them as to
us to come out of nowhere. But they are all afraid to speak;
too polite. Perhaps if they say nothing, it will go away.
JACOB clears his throat purposefully. Finally LEAH,
not quite believing the others' silence, helps HEIDI out.)*

LEAH: *The Color Purple?*

HEIDI: That's the one. I could name you a dozen better
novels published in any year that will sink like stones
while students are force-fed this second-rate work.
It all goes back to what I said before. We are afraid to
say what's true. Somewhere along the line, we stopped
being a ruling elite, became terribly self-conscious.
Vietnam wounded us, Nixon twisted the knife, and
then the culture of money came along and buried us.
Who's running this country now, does anyone know?
Is it one of those wormy little men whose faces I'm
forced to look at just because he affected a great merger
or cornered the market on micro chips? All I know
is it's not us anymore. Not us with our standards and
our decency—

FRANK: *(Trying to silence her)* Heidi, you're overwrought.

HEIDI: *(visibly upset now)* No I'm not. I detest Christmas.
Detest this holly.

LEAH: *(Rising)* Jacob, I think we should go. We told
Noah we'd be home by ten.

JACOB: But it's barely—

LEAH: I'll get the coats, okay? *(She exits.)*

MARGARET: *(Sensitive to be being left with JACOB)* Yes,
it's time for me to go, too.

HEIDI: *(As soon as* MARGARET's *left)* I'm afraid I've
emptied out the room.

AARON: No, Heidi, it's just that the Maid Marion Opus
won't wait. *(He looks at the others, expecting smiles.)*

JACOB: *(Hard)* Excuse me.

AARON: Yes?

JACOB: What did you mean by that?

AARON: *(Amazed that he should be called on this)* A joke.
That's all *(Beat. Perhaps a jab)* We all know how hard
Margaret is trying to justify her own behavior by
finding one instance from history.

JACOB: *(Beat. Still an effort)* Why don't you take that back.

AARON: *(Beat. Mildly outraged)* Jacob.

JACOB: Why don't you —take that back. It's an insult
to her and I—find I can't allow that.

AARON: Well, Jacob, this is new.

JACOB: Maybe. Yes. But I'm asking you to take that back.

AARON: *(After a moment's perusal of* JACOB*)* Why don't
you have another cigar, Jacob

*(*JACOB *tries to hit him.* FRANK *holds him back.)*

FRANK: Good God.

*(*LEAH *enters, with coats. She sees only the end of this.)*

LEAH: What—are you fighting about? Please? I hope it's
what she said. I hope you're not still silent. This woman
has just insulted an entire race and its literature, and
you—what are you fighting about?

*(*MARGARET *enters, in her coat, having heard, of course,
everything, but pretending she hasn't.)*

MARGARET: Thank you, Heidi. It was a lovely evening.

HEIDI: *(To both* LEAH *and* MARGARET:*)* I had so hoped we could sing one carol as a group. Won't you stay for just that?

LEAH: The car will be frozen on a night like this. I'll warm it up. *(She drops* JACOB's *coat for him, exits.)*

HEIDI: *(In defeat)* Well, perhaps I'll get that started. One carol. Anyone?

(There are no takers. At the last moment, HEIDI *takes* CHRIS' *hand, leading him helplessly out with her.)*

MARGARET: *(To the others, difficult)* Well, goodnight then. *(Exits)*

AARON: A Christmas carol sounds appropriate right about now. Peace on earth. I'm very aware the rules are changing, Jacob, but I wasn't aware they're changing quite this fast. A little joke among friends.

(He exits. Somewhere near the end of his speech, the group in the next room, led by HEIDI, *begins to sing* Angels We Have Heard On High. *A raggedy beginning, which gradually coalesces, and continues through the end of the act.)*

NICOLE: Closer to understanding one another. I wonder. Come to my house some morning, or evening. Listen to the bears growl. Watch the news. What should we be teaching them, Jacob? *(She, too, exits.)*

*(*JACOB *and* FRANK *alone)*

FRANK: Are you—*mad*? Trying to hit our chairman? Would you like to be teaching six sections of Freshman Comp next semester?

JACOB: Why not?

FRANK: Is it so bad? Has it gotten so bad that you are willing to give up what you've worked to achieve?

JACOB: What, Frank, have I worked to achieve? A strait-jacket? Something feels alive, that's all. God, we should be fighting more. Taking off our jackets and stepping outside more. Goodnight, Frank.

(His coat on, JACOB *exits. Set goes to black, with only light at the front of the stage. Light snow falling.* JACOB *has stepped outside from out of the shadows,* MARGARET *appears, having waited for him.)*

JACOB: You heard everything, didn't you? God, I can't stand to see you hurt.

*(*JACOB *tries to go to* MARGARET. *She motions for him to stop, takes a step back herself.)*

MARGARET: Hold on to something, please. Hold on to a little of what you were. *(Beat)* I'm getting frightened.

JACOB: Why? *(Truly incredulous)* Why?

(Offstage, a car horn honks, his signal from LEAH. *He waits a moment, then goes. From within the party,* Angels We Have Heard on High *reaches a crescendo.* MARGARET *stands looking after him, in the light snow.)*

END OF ACT ONE

ACT TWO

Scene One

(JACOB's *office*)

(*It is late January, the start of the second semester.* JACOB *is at his desk, and* WENDY, *his student from* ACT ONE, *is seated beside him, leaning forward, very intense.*)

WENDY: I keep going back to the first moment. When he touched her breasts, or whatever— (*Beat*) It's embarrassing, but, what happens when a man looks at a woman and decides he wants her?

(JACOB *looks at* WENDY, *but doesn't speak.*)

WENDY: You're not going to tell me. Whatever it is, it happened. He went in her. He ejaculated. Who knows what he was thinking? Probably about some other woman, and she—I bet for her it was something like, what was she going to make him for lunch the next day. And there, you know, I began. (*Beat. Thoughtful*) There couldn't have been love there. I *know* that. Otherwise things would have turned out differently.

(CHRIS *enters, in hat and coat, covered with snow.*)

CHRIS: 'Morning.

JACOB: You're covered with snow.

CHRIS: (*As if he hasn't noticed*) Am I? Yes. Been walking. (*He looks at* JACOB. *As if he has to coax himself to say it:*) Had the ultrasound this morning. (*The flicker of a smile*

*appears on his face, the first time we've seen him smile. He's
filled with an embarrassed awe he can't hold back.)* They
hold a kind of—camera, over the mound— and you see,
on a screen, the thing, *moving. (He starts to demonstrate.
Then, in the midst of it, he stops, scratches his nose.)* Well,
it's not important. *(He quickly removes his hat and coat,
then rushes to his desk, as if to duck* JACOB's *questions.)*

JACOB: So? See a little penis flopping around?

CHRIS: *(At his desk, to work)* It was turned the other way.

WENDY: Professor Freundlich?

JACOB: *(Recalled)* Oh, yes, sorry. You were recreating the
circumstances of your conception.

WENDY: *(Testing him)* Are you taking this seriously?

JACOB: You know, in my curious way, I am.

(The phone rings. Both JACOB *and* CHRIS *are excited at the
possibility it represents.)*

CHRIS: I'll—

JACOB: *(Quicker)* No. I'm expecting a call. *(To* WENDY*)*
Sorry. *(Into phone:)* Hello? *(Disappointed, covering it:)*
Oh yes, he's here. No, he hasn't shown me any pictures.
He didn't even tell me he had any with him. Here he is.

*(*JACOB *gestures to* CHRIS *to pick up his phone, then hangs
up.)*

JACOB: Your wife. Pictures of the ultrasound? *(Back to*
WENDY, *apologetic)* These interruptions.

WENDY: *(Holding back, self-protectively)* It's okay.
I should probably shut up anyway. I guess it's time
to realize this whole project, this trying to prove we
don't know our own souls, it's just a way to try and
justify my father's character. Professor Freundlich,
he's a man who couldn't stay. He's had four wives.
Six children. He's got a twenty six year old girlfriend

now. He just keeps repeating the same faithlessness, and I don't understand how he can not *see* himself.

CHRIS: *(Into phone)* Yes. I was moved as well.

WENDY: I thought if I could find enough books showing he wasn't really to blame, then maybe I could forgive him. But these books document hopelessness. If Kafka is the truth, if Bernhard is the truth, how do people find the strength to get out of bed in the morning?

(Beat. JACOB looks at WENDY.)

JACOB: Well, usually we have to pee. The needs of the bladder are God's answer to Eastern European literature.

(In spite of herself, WENDY has begun to laugh.)

WENDY: No. It's not funny.

JACOB: Well, but maybe in a way it is. *(He considers her.)* I mean, I think I can appreciate the amount of pain your father's faithlessness has caused you. Or maybe I can't. Maybe I'm just being presumptuous. But he's human— he's not *you*. That is—well, what am I saying? You can't find forgiveness in books. *(He rejects that.)* You can't construct a theory that will allow you to live. Life evades theory. Your father—look, you want the basic truth? We walk on either side of a line—either we have children and deny ourselves, or else we live for ourselves and basically deny our children. Is this harsh?

WENDY: Yes. But I think I need to hear it.

(WENDY nods. While JACOB is talking, CHRIS hangs up the phone, takes the picture of the fetus out of his wallet, lays it on his desk in front of him. This should be fairly surreptitious; it is not meant to point up or comment on what JACOB is saying, save in the most oblique way.)

JACOB: Sometimes a child is so real to you—I feel this as they get older, especially my older son, my

daughter—that in the moment of just looking at them
the rest of life stops. You say, and you mean it, this is
all there is.

WENDY: And you're saying my father never felt that
way for me.

JACOB: No, I'm not saying that. Even if your father felt
it, how could he go through every second of his life
saying "My child is all there is?" He simply—made
another move.

(Beat. A moment where JACOB *might be about to reveal
more.* WENDY *picks up on it.)*

WENDY: So you struggle with this, too.

JACOB: *(Suddenly embarrassed, he backs off.)* Well.
These are questions we all ask. That's all.

WENDY: Intellectual questions.

JACOB: Yes.

WENDY: I wish you'd tell me if they were more than
that. I wish you'd let me in. These questions affect
my life. *(It becomes too much for her. Very suddenly,
without warning, she starts to cry.)* I'm sorry. The last
thing I wanted to do in here today was cry. I'm sorry.

JACOB: It's all right. It's okay. Oh, come on.

*(*JACOB *puts his arm around* WENDY *in an attempt to
comfort her, just as* HOMER *steps into the office covered
with snow and holding a sheaf of papers.)*

HOMER: Good God, take your hands off her, Jacob,
before the Army of Militant Lesbian Feminists get
wind of this! *(He slams the door dramatically, as if
defending the room from attack.)*

JACOB: She's upset.

HOMER: She's upset? *I'm* upset. Come over here for a
cup of tea, you'd think I was a spreader of the Plague.

None of them over in our department office would
say a word to me.

JACOB: You're not supposed to be on campus.

HOMER: Don't you think I know that? Had to get
my mail, didn't I? Not that it matters. Load of bloody
nonsense. *(Reading from the papers in his hand:)* "Students
to Witness Haiti's Agony", well isn't that wonderful.
"Professor Morris Rigby of Yale will lecture on
"Authenticity in *The Merry Wives of Windsor*".
Won't want to miss that one, will you? "Friends of
Rowing invites you to..." Well now, who in bloody
hell *are* the Friends of Rowing, and why do they feel
suddenly compelled to declare their friendliness?
Did I miss something epochal in the history of Rowing?
(He drops the entire sheaf, the rest unread, into JACOB's
wastebasket, sinks into a chair.) No forgiveness. No respite.

JACOB: *(To* WENDY*)* Can I get you something? A cup of
tea?

WENDY: Yes please.

HOMER: What's the matter with this one?

JACOB: A faithless Dad. I'll be right back

HOMER: Get me a cup of tea, too, would you, Jacob?
Department Secretary practically yanked the box of
tea bags out of my hand. Just don't tell her it's for me.

*(*JACOB *exits.* HOMER *rises, stands awkwardly above*
WENDY, *who is sitting.)*

HOMER: Ah well. You're all right, then?

*(*HOMER *touches* WENDY's *shoulder. The act,
sympathetically intended, and not thought about
beforehand—a natural gesture—suddenly seems charged
with significance, and he lifts his hand off, puts it in his
pocket, as if he has come to see his own natural inclinations
as dangerous things.)*

WENDY: You're Professor Boykin, aren't you?

HOMER: I am. Yes.

WENDY: That was a shitty thing you did to Nikki Gallagher.

HOMER: Was it? Yes.

WENDY: She was traumatized by it.

HOMER: Tell her I'm sorry then, won't you?

WENDY: I don't think sorry is enough.

HOMER: *(Beat. A distraction:)* What's that you're looking at, Chris?

CHRIS: *(Covering the picture of his baby, which has been distracting him.)* Look, I'm sorry, but I can't compromise myself. The ruling is, you're not allowed on campus.

(FRANK enters, holding papers.)

FRANK: Jacob, I need to— *(Notices* HOMER*)* Homer, you're not supposed to be here.

HOMER: Yes, apparently there's no defense from the Jack the Ripper of Faculty Lane.

FRANK: If that student were to see you, she might be set back in her recovery.

HOMER: What's there to recover from? Somebody tell me please.

WENDY: *(Rising, gathering her books)* I don't think I should be hearing this.

FRANK: No, you shouldn't.

WENDY: Would you tell Professor Freundlich I'd like to drop this Independent? Tell him it's not his fault, but I don't really feel equipped to handle soullessness. *(Beat)* Tell him—tell him thanks, though. *(She exits.)*

HOMER: *(A question)* Frank.

FRANK: *(Deflecting)* Please tell Jacob I'd like a word with him when he gets back.

HOMER: Frank, the Committee's decision's been put off to late in May. About me, I mean.

FRANK: Yes. It has.

HOMER: Why, Frank?

FRANK: It was felt—

HOMER: I don't like sentences in the passive voice. Someone felt. Some individual felt. And talked others into. Let's be straight.

FRANK: All of us on the Committee felt it's far too sensitive an issue to deal with during the school year. It would distract the students.

HOMER: So May. *Late* May.

FRANK: When the students are gone, yes.

HOMER: When those who might stand up in my defense are gone, anyway. I'm dead then, is what you're saying.

FRANK: We all have open minds, Homer. However, I feel it's only fair to warn you there are passionate people on this committee.

(JACOB enters, carrying two cups of tea.)

JACOB: Here we are. Nice hot— Where is she?

HOMER: She's dropping the Independent.

(JACOB looks out into the hall for WENDY. Too late)

HOMER: I'll take my tea, Jacob.

JACOB: She just left? Did she leave a message?

FRANK: Jacob, I'd like to talk to you.

HOMER: Finish, Frank. Passionate people.

FRANK: Yes, well, you know how hot an issue this has become. Time was, if a man was a good man, and tried to fondle a tit from time to time, nothing was done about it. A slap of the hand, if that.

HOMER: The women have come into power, yes.

FRANK: *(As if this pains him)* I will try to make every argument in your defense that I possibly can.

HOMER: *(Sipping his tea)* And will you talk about the tits you've fondled, Frank?

FRANK: *(Beat)* I don't think so.

HOMER: That ridiculous pregnancy how many years back?

FRANK: Many.

HOMER: Everyone knew about it. Still, you weren't punished.

FRANK: No, I wasn't. It's stupid to say I suffered, of course. But I did. Still, I wasn't punished. It would be hypocritical of me to bring in the word unfairness here.

HOMER: Good for you. Bloody good for you. Yes, the air is full of fine sentiments this morning. What I want to know is, what are any of you going to do about it?

FRANK: We are— Sorry, I am going to argue as vehemently in your favor as I possibly can.

(FRANK clears his throat. HOMER does a mock double-take.)

FRANK: I'm not against you, I find. I don't know how these others feel, but all of this puritanical nonsense seems to me a grand distraction from our true business, which some people seem to have forgotten is to educate. Against what might be a part of my better judgment, I find myself your advocate on Committee.

HOMER: *(Has to take a moment just to take this in.)* Well, bravo. Yes, bravo.

FRANK: Now if you don't mind, I'd like to talk to Jacob. Alone.

HOMER: Oh, I don't mind. You're speaking the truth, are you?

FRANK: I am.

HOMER: *(Still with a grain of suspicion)* I'm trusting you, Frank.

FRANK: I'm aware of that.

HOMER: But about the May decision—

FRANK: *(Firm)* I can argue for you in Committee. I can't help you with the timing. Just—sweat it out.

HOMER: *(Something occurs to him)* Sweat it out. Yes. Thanks for the tea, Jacob. *(He exits.)*

JACOB: *(Looks at* FRANK *a long moment)* You shameless hussy. Every word of that was a lie, wasn't it?

FRANK: Every word, I'm afraid.

JACOB: Frank, we're sophisticated men. We're cynical men of the world. But to lie to Homer at this point?

FRANK: If I told him the truth, I'd never hear the end of it, would I? He'd bring up that poor girl I got pregnant twenty years ago. Not that there was anything to that. She went on to have a fine career, a family—no lasting harm was done. But if it were to come out in this climate, I couldn't show my face around here. This way, we do it in May, he can make all the stink he wants, no one will be here to hear it.

JACOB: *(After considering all this for a moment, unhappily)* What did you want to see me about?

FRANK: Our Appointments meeting. *(He turns to* CHRIS.*)* Chris, if you don't mind, this should take only a moment.

CHRIS: *(Looks annoyedly at* FRANK*)* Some coffee. *(He exits.)*

FRANK: Well, it's shameful. And let's take care of the racism issue right away. My point is not a racist point, and don't try to make it one. We have settled on two candidates, one of them very good, entirely viable, a jewel in the Department's crown, and the other— well, let us just say her reputation precedes her. *(He hands* JACOB *a vita.)* She has written a book— you've heard of it—whose relation to serious scholarship eludes me. Perhaps others here feel that what's been lacking all along in our Department is a good healthy concentration on American voodoo rites, but I can't say I'm in agreement.

JACOB: *(Recognizing the name on the vita)* That's not really what the book was about.

FRANK: We can argue that at another time. The problem now is that she is a black woman, and therefore a very hot ticket. A black woman with a national reputation. No one is seeing the issue in front of us and I am having a *very* hard time convincing people that a woman— albeit a white woman—who has written an excellent new book on the Harlem Renaissance is at least the equal of the author of *Delta Priestesses*.

JACOB: So what did you come to me for?

FRANK: Well, I have a small problem. You see, I have to vote for her.

JACOB: For?

FRANK: *(Tapping the vita)* This Lila Golden. The black woman.

JACOB: You don't have to keep calling her "the black woman".

*(*FRANK *raises an eyebrow.)*

JACOB: You have to vote for her because...?

FRANK: Because my wife opened her mouth at our Christmas party. Those awful racist Leech's, both of whom have been contributing to the United Negro College Fund since 1963. Now I've done some basic arithmetic. Given our Department, I'd say that even without my vote there is a slim chance this woman who wrote the Harlem Renaissance book— *(He hands* JACOB *a second vita.)* can prevail. Now here's what I propose. You give your assurance that when the Department votes, you'll back my candidate, and I'll give you Homer.

JACOB: You'll give *me*—? *(Beat)* Why would you do this?

FRANK: He's the lesser of two evils, I'm afraid. In any case, he'll be gone in a few years, by which point this Lila Golden will be, I trust, gainfully employed somewhere else. *(Beat)* Now I know for a fact that you don't care so awfully much about these diversity issues. You've never spoken of them once in my presence. So this is an opportunity for you to save your friend.

JACOB: Frank, how much power do you have on this committee?

FRANK: A great deal, as it happens. At least, as far as the punishment. And he *will* be punished. But as to whether Homer is completely cut out or given some more moderate censure, I believe I do have that much power.

JACOB: Why don't you give me some time on this.

FRANK: Time? What do you need time for? *(He chuckles.)* Jacob, have you developed a social conscience overnight? *(Beat. Realizing the need for delicacy:)* I'm sorry. Of course you can have time. Menwhile, I'll leave these with you.

(A moment where they just look at each other, each trying to figure the other out. Then FRANK *exits.)*

*(*JACOB *sits alone a moment, in thought.* HOMER *re-enters.)*

HOMER: I don't trust him as far as I can throw him.

JACOB: No. You shouldn't.

HOMER: It was all a lie, then?

JACOB: That's the funny thing. Frank is prepared to help you out. *(Beat. A consideration.)* Tell me the truth. Tell me what happened. It's very important that I know.

*(*HOMER *sits. Silence, with the two of them locked into one another.)*

HOMER: I went too far. *(Beat)*

JACOB: Yes?

HOMER: Nothing she won't recover from. Still— *(Beat)* I touched her knee, that's all. *(He clears his throat.)*

JACOB: Are you sure?

HOMER: Perhaps a little more. *(Beat)* Moment of desperation, really. For an instant, it seemed the whole world was right there. *(Beat)* A bit more. A bit higher I got before she pulled away. *(Beat)* The problem wasn't in the touch, Jacob. The problem was in what I did when I saw she was going to get up and go. I tried to keep her there in the room with me. *(Beat)* I used force. *(Beat)* Foolish.

*(*JACOB *is intent on him.* HOMER *looks up and meets* JACOB'S *eyes.)*

JACOB: Would you like to walk me to class?

HOMER: I would like that, yes. The campus feels more like home to me than home.

*(*JACOB *gets up and puts on his coat and scarf.)*

HOMER: Why did you want to know all this?

JACOB: *(An awkward moment. He is searching for something.)* You were always very good to me. When I started here. You helped me out.

(HOMER appears lost.)

JACOB: Come on.

(They exit together. Empty office for a moment. Then CHRIS and AARON enter, in mid-conversation.)

AARON: —we'd have to put the call out for an additional person, we've got a whole new search, a whole new ball game. The numbers are not that compelling. Richard speaks Spanish. We just stick them up in his classes, or add—

(They've been walking to CHRIS' desk. AARON finds the ultrasound picture.)

AARON: What's this?

CHRIS: *(Taking the picture back)* My kid.

AARON: Ha. *(Considers CHRIS appreciatively.)* Ha. *(Beat)* I'm very lonely, you know.

(AARON puts his hand on CHRIS' shoulder, kneads the skin. CHRIS knocks the hand away.)

AARON: Boy or girl?

CHRIS: Don't know.

AARON: *(Beat)* Look, E S L is not the most pressing of my concerns. *(He starts out.)*

CHRIS: *(Stopping him verbally)* I meant that. No calls in the night. No calls. I won't *meet* you. My wife begins to get upset. She knows about us. I am with her now. I won't be with you any longer.

AARON: *(Not upset)* I get your message, Chris. *(He exits.)*

(CHRIS *stares at the door. A confused look of longing and regret; he opens his mouth as if a scream wants to come out. Then he picks up the picture of his child, holds it up at arm's length, walks around the room staring at it. In the midst of this,* JACOB *comes in.*)

JACOB: Forgot something.

(CHRIS, *embarrassed, hides the picture, goes to work at his desk.* JACOB *knows he's caught* CHRIS *at something, but has a more urgent intention. He goes to his phone, dials. When he speaks, it's a* JACOB *we haven't heard before, save for the peek we got at this side of him at the end of* ACT ONE: JACOB *in love.*)

JACOB: Listen. Hi. Hi. You didn't call me. No. I'll be a few minutes late, is that all right? Yes. Yes. Of course. Yes.

(*Beat.* JACOB *hangs up. A moment where he's in his own world. Then he finds the book he "needs", and holds it up as an excuse for* CHRIS. *He looks at* CHRIS *a moment, knows that something is up, just as* CHRIS, *overhearing the illicit phone conversation, knows something is up with* JACOB.)

JACOB: You all right?

CHRIS: (*No response.*) Of course.

(JACOB *decides not to pursue it. He exits.* CHRIS *looks after him, perhaps wondering for a moment, then takes out the picture, lays it before him as he returns to work.*)

(*Lights fade.*)

Scene Two

(MARGARET's house)

(Late evening in Spring. Blossoms on the tree. Crickets)

(JACOB appears, dressed for a party. He looks up at the unlit house.)

JACOB: *(A voice of cautious longing)* Margaret! *(There is no answer. Louder, needier:)* Margaret? Are you awake?

(A light goes on inside. After a moment, MARGARET appears at the door, in a nightgown.)

MARGARET: *(From inside.)* Is that you? I was sleeping.

JACOB: Why weren't you at the party?

MARGARET: *(Opening the door, but not inviting him in.)* I don't know. Decided not to go. *(Beat)* It must be late.

JACOB: *(Gazing up at the trees.)* Look at this. It's Spring! "It's Spring and all Spring means." What's that from? *(Hits himself on the forehead, to stop himself.)* God, why am I always quoting people? You'd think there'd be some words—in *here*—some actual words of my *own*.

MARGARET: You're drunk, aren't you?

(JACOB looks around her yard, suddenly lost.)

MARGARET: What is it? What's the matter?

JACOB: My son knows.

MARGARET: How?

JACOB: *(To downplay it:)* Nothing. Nothing. I was— the other night—leaving, to come here. His window is just above the driveway. I've been escaping that house to come here—what? Six months? —But that night, I don't know, I must have had some *look* on me. He gazed at me from his window. We had this—*moment*. I think he was asking for the first time: who *is* this guy? (*Beat. He takes in what is, for him, the enormity of this recollected moment.*) Let me in, please.

MARGARET: Drunk and sad? Think it'd be any good? (*She comes out, sits on the porch, invites him to join her.*) Come. Sit here.

JACOB: (*Trying to make up for something.*) I'm not sad. I'm not—. Seeing you-. No. (*Beat. He doesn't sit. He experiences a moment of helplessness. A change of subject, away from pain:*) I've got this decision to make, Margaret. I want you to help me.

MARGARET: What's that?

JACOB: Frank wants me to make a deal. He wants my vote for his Ethnic Studies candidate.

MARGARET: In exchange for—?

JACOB: Homer.

MARGARET: Is that so very complicated? Frank wants to defeat Lila Golden, that goes without saying.
  But you can't go along with it.

JACOB: (*Unconvinced, his mind elsewhere*) Yes.

MARGARET: We can't bring minority students here and ask them to function in a totally white environment. You must know that.

JACOB: I do. Yes.

MARGARET: Besides which, she'd be an incredible breath of fresh air for all of us.

JACOB: (*Beat*) You look very beautiful.

MARGARET: Half asleep? But thank you. I had a nice night.

JACOB: Alone?

MARGARET: A glass of wine. A book. You know that Gerry Stern poem, *This Was A Wonderful Night*?

JACOB: No.

MARGARET: The fourth line is "No one called".

JACOB: *(Beat)* This is what you want, then?

MARGARET: I think so.

JACOB: To be alone. To have lovers.

MARGARET: A lover.

JACOB: Someone to dance for you.

(Beat. MARGARET looks at JACOB a moment, wondering if he means by that something facetious, possibly cruel. They each decide to let it sit, not to follow it up.)

JACOB: So you think—you think it would be wrong to try and save Homer?

MARGARET: Yes I do. I can't believe you'd even consider—

JACOB: *(Not letting her finish)* It seems a little cowardly, that's all. Too easy, I mean. Frank is right. I never *think* about these things. Who's on the faculty. The color of our skins and whether we're sufficiently sensitized to our own *whiteness*. What is this? I mean, we're talking about *Homer*.

MARGARET: Yes, we are. But we're also talking about something more than Homer. *(Becoming slightly exasperated)* You can't have men like Homer Boykin let loose on American campuses anymore. We teach young *women*, Jacob. They have the right to go into a conference without the risk of getting mauled.

JACOB: Look, I concede the political issue. I really do. There *is* no question. But you don't just throw a man away because he *slips*.

MARGARET: No? I would think keeping your hands to yourself would be a simple enough requisite at a women's college.

JACOB: *(Himself becoming exasperated. He knows his arguments have only an emotional merit)* What are we *standing* for here? If not...the life of *feeling*, that's what we teach, isn't it?

MARGARET: *(Taking a careful tack with him, seeing where he's going)* Not entirely. No. I don't think I need to remind you that what we teach, what literature teaches, is the *conflict* of the moral life with the life of feeling.

JACOB: Oh shut up. Here we are having an academic discussion and all I want to do is say, Christ, take off your clothes and let me hold you.

MARGARET: *(Beat)* I don't think so. Not tonight.

JACOB: Why not? Why not? *(When she doesn't answer:)* Because you're afraid? *(Beat. He comes closer, takes her hand.)* You know what I'm afraid of? That we won't... we might not...recognize *this*...as maybe... *(He can't quite say it.)*

MARGARET: What?

JACOB: I've been so happy lately, just trotting around, saying "I'm in love, I'm in love". And then this morning, I passed the mirror in the bathroom and got one of those looks at myself, the ones where you're not posing and you see the total horror of your physical existence at a glance, and I thought: she loves *this*? *(Beat. Exultant:)* But I feel like—for the first time in my life—I'm at a place where I can stop looking at myself. And maybe— *(The exultancy takes him to another place. It's as though he's about to cry now, his joy intersecting with the hugeness of his desire. He's frightened of it, and he backs off.)*

MARGARET: *(Recognizing what's going on; careful.)*
I didn't want it to go this far.

JACOB: No.

MARGARET: I can't trust— *(Beat. Very hard for her)*
—a man who comes to me in the night, the first thing
he says to me is, My son knows.

JACOB: *(Trying to defuse it)* That was—

MARGARET: That was what? Would that ever disappear?

*(Beat. A long moment where he takes that in, fighting it in
silence.)*

JACOB: *(Quietly, almost as though he's distracted.)* So,
you think I have to vote for this Lila Golden.

MARGARET: *(Equally quiet)* Yes.

JACOB: *(In the same mode.)* I sometimes think, me, a
white man, with black students, how much do I have
to— *(He starts to weep, silently.)* —give them. *(Beat)* Sorry.

MARGARET: No.

JACOB: Sorry. *(Beat. Slowly, finally, hesitantly he goes
to her, nestles himself like a child with his face in her lap.)*
I want to go inside you. Not what you're thinking.
Not sex. Just to go to that place, where I have no son,
no life. Only this. Why isn't that possible? Only this.
Please take me inside. For more than just a moment.
Please.

MARGARET: *(Beat. She cradles him. Her own difficulty:)*
If I felt— If I just once felt— Do you understand that
I can't, that I am too old to—. My *heart*, you know?
Once I lay down on the floor and screamed because
a man was leaving me. Screamed. Couldn't get up.
Thought—death. Thought—a knife, a rope, because
someone else had the power to do that to me. *(Beat)*
If you make me go to that place again, you have to
be willing to stay.

(Beat. JACOB *touches* MARGARET's *face, then slowly kisses her, pulls her down. They lie on the porch, beginning to make love.)*

(Lights fade on them, as, on the opposite side of the stage, LEAH *appears, in a pool of light.)*

Scene Three

(Outside JACOB's *house)*

(It's late, LEAH *is in a robe, her hair is slightly messy. She looks up at the sky, arms folded against the chill of the night.)*

*(*JACOB *appears, carrying a small mattress.)*

LEAH: Whose?

JACOB: Joe's. I left him the box spring.

LEAH: The box spring.

JACOB: I told him I'd buy him a new one tomorrow.

LEAH: *(Nods)* So. There. Goodbye.

JACOB: *(He rests the mattress.)* You want me to be honest with you. *(Beat)* You don't want falseness, Leah. It's been our deal from the beginning.

LEAH: Yes. God forbid.

JACOB: *(Probing)* What?

LEAH: *Go.* Don't stay. Take your mattress.

JACOB: What? I can't stand it. I know that look on your face. Something to say.

*(*LEAH *shakes her head.)*

JACOB: Say it.

LEAH: When did you become such a creature of principles, that's what I'm wondering. My *shlub* husband. Falseness. Dishonesty. Men have affairs. It's

pathetic, but it happens. Why can't you skulk around
and feel guilty like everybody else?

JACOB: You want me to *stay*?

LEAH: I don't know what I want. I look at you and
I feel—it's pathetic. I don't know if I want you to stay.
What you're doing is wrong. This is not a moment
of selflessness I'm having here. It's wrong for *you*.
You'll suffer. All right. Now go.

JACOB: We made a deal—

LEAH: *(Overlapping on "deal", as if she's anticipating him)*
What, marriage is a "deal"? We shake hands? Once
things go a certain way we stop? Because—what?—
We're corrupted? Give me Joe's mattress. *(She grabs it
from him, close to violence.)* I will not have a nine year
old boy sleeping on a box spring.

JACOB: *(Beat)* I can't take the box spring. It won't fold.
It won't fit in the car.

LEAH: Then sleep on the floor. Sleep on a bed of nails.
You love your own darkness. Punish yourself, it's what
you want.

*(LEAH holds the mattress as if it's something she can
hold between them. They look at each other. A shift.
The conversation moves to a level where it might seem
more casual, as if they are not fighting.)*

LEAH: So.

JACOB: *(Looks at her a long moment, waiting for more
to come.)* I'm wondering—what would it be I'd be
punishing myself for?

LEAH: *(Quiet, tired.)* Go. Get out of here.

(JACOB waits.)

LEAH: That things went right. That you were blessed.
That none of your children got sick, or died, or was

born wrong. That I didn't die. That you didn't fail.
Or lose an arm. Or get cancer. Because any of those
things would keep you here. Would make you
interesting to yourself. It's not about her. Is it? This.

JACOB: I don't know. Sometimes I don't think so.
How do you *know* this?

LEAH: I knew more about you in the first five minutes
than you've learned in the past eighteen years. You
don't care as much about women as you're trying to
convince me. Eighteen years of monogamy and now
this? Do you think for a second you were made for
that kind of happiness?

JACOB: *(Beat. It's a real question)* I don't know.

LEAH: It's late. I'm going to bring Joe his mattress.

JACOB: Why aren't you more angry with me? Why are
you being decent?

LEAH: I could kill you. But I'm not being betrayed here.
Other men, yes, they betray their wives, but you—
it's different. I'm watching a man who's lost, that's all.
*(Beat. She's about to go, having said what she needed to say,
but can't resist adding one more thing.)* Why did you let
yourself get so bored?

JACOB: I don't know. I had to keep this job. We needed
money, we had children.

LEAH: Yes. And now you've found the solution to all of
that, haven't you. *(Beat. One final look at him)* You'll feel
for the rest of your life like half of yourself.

*(LEAH exits. JACOB watches her. Alone, he's scared by what
she just said. The he, too, exits, in the opposite direction.)*

(JACOB's office. Graduation night)

*(Opening music: the bells of the college chapel play a
graduation anthem. Lights out in JACOB's office. Dark.
Laughter. Figures at the door, trying to open it.)*

JACOB: *(In the dark)* ...author of such and such and such and such and do you remember the names of any of her books?

MARGARET: Unfortunately, not a one.

(Finally, the key works. JACOB *and* MARGARET *enter. He stumbles to his desk to find a light.)*

JACOB: Well, they must have had success in their time, but the poor old ancient black novelist is only up on that graduation stage because this institution needs to make a yearly show of its progressive view of race—

*(*JACOB *finds his desk lamp and turns it on. We can see now that both he and* MARGARET *are wearing their graduation robes, bright and colorful as befitting their doctorates. He is carrying a bottle of champagne, which they have been drinking from. They are in giddy moods.)*

JACOB: And Frank Leech, who has done everything in his power to keep Lila Golden—

MARGARET: A vital and *young* black woman.

JACOB: —from getting hired here, is up there holding hands with this poor old crone, looking like Lyndon Johnson signing the Voting Rights Act. The air of self-congratulation was so thick you could—

MARGARET: Cut it with a knife. Yes. Some more of that, please.

(She holds out her glass. JACOB *fills it.)*

JACOB: Until everyone realizes, my God, she's taking out a *speech*. She thinks we want her to *talk*.

MARGARET: Instead of just up there on stage as a figurehead.

JACOB: Right. I mean, imagine, this relic from the past, what would she have to say to us?

MARGARET: "Look on my works, ye mighty, and despair"?

JACOB: At *least* that. But no, no, figurehead only. Until suddenly—

(JACOB *begins acting out the scene, to* MARGARET'*s delight.*)

JACOB: —she begins moving toward the podium, holding the longest graduation speech in the history of the world. And Frank Leech is tugging at her robes, pulling her back to her seat—

MARGARET: No speech, no speech!

JACOB: And the President, quick as a whip, introduces the afternoon's true honoree—

MARGARET: Jodie Foster!

JACOB: Who was inspiring, wasn't she?

(*Outside the window, a display of fireworks has started. Vivid, spectacular, it plays against the glass of the window.* MARGARET *notices before* JACOB.)

MARGARET: Oh look. (*She goes to the window, stands there watching, entranced.*)

JACOB: Yes, it's a big night for all our girls.

MARGARET: Wouldn't it be wonderful, just for one night, to not have to make fun of all this? (*She turns to him.*) Come here, Jacob.

(JACOB *does.* MARGARET *kisses him, very slowly and deeply.*)

(*They break apart. A moment of complicated feeling on* JACOB'*s part.*)

MARGARET: Oh, that wasn't very good. We can do better.

(*The sound of laughter in the hall.* HEIDI *and* FRANK.)

HEIDI: Do I see a light on? *(She peeks her head in.)* You missed dinner with Jodie Foster.

MARGARET: Yes. Deliberately.

HEIDI: Oh, she was just as cold and snippy as you'd expect, but how often do you get to have dinner with a genuine movie star? *(Calling into the hallway:)* Frank, Jacob and Margaret are here!

FRANK: *(Voice, offstage)* Are they?

HEIDI: Bring the wine in here, Frank. *(Turning back to them, she moves to the window.)* Oh, look at those fireworks. They do give them a lovely sendoff, don't they?

(They watch the fireworks display. HEIDI notices CHRIS's desk.)

HEIDI: Where was Chris today?

JACOB: He called me this morning. Carole went into labor.

(FRANK enters, in his robes, which are far more spectacular than either JACOB's or MARGARET's.)

JACOB: *(Bowing)* Cardinal Woolsey, I presume.

FRANK: I've got this lovely bottle of wine. Would you like some?

MARGARET: Oh yes, please. What is it?

HEIDI: Who cares? It's old and it's French.

FRANK: *(Reading the label)* Gevrey-Chambertin. I don't know wines, but I do know that J P Donleavy thinks highly of this one. Mentions it in his books. The early ones. The good ones. *(He pours the wine and disperses it.)*

HEIDI: *(Still at the window, the continuing fireworks display playing against her face.)* Oh, I feel old tonight. I feel ancient.

FRANK: You're very young.

HEIDI: Thank you, Frank, but I'm not. And I don't want
to be in their places. Just finding a man. Or looking.
All that self-doubt. The only advantage of youth,
I suppose, is that if you're lucky you have slim thighs.

FRANK: Your thighs, Heidi, are barely discernible.
Now what are we drinking to?

HEIDI: To the graduating students.

FRANK: Spoiled brats, every one. Something more
worthy, Heidi.

JACOB: To Jodie Foster!

HEIDI: Oh no, look, I have it. Let's drink to *duty* and
order , and age and loss, all those marvelous concepts
that are such antidotes to this magic in the air.

FRANK: Oh, let's just drink, for God's sake. *(They do.)*

MARGARET: Mm. Very good.

FRANK: Yes. Yes, it is. Heidi, I wish you wouldn't use
phrases like "magic in the air". It makes you sound like
an ingénue.

HEIDI: I don't mind sounding like an *ingénue*.

JACOB: Are you thinking of running off on old Frank,
Heidi?

HEIDI: Well, there were all these young men around
tonight. I don't know what it is about the young.
They're not more attractive than older men, but
you almost never want to bite a man of forty.

JACOB: *(Delighted by this)* Did you want to bite someone?

HEIDI: Oh yes. One in particular. He looked so
wonderful. Not really good looking. Chunky, you'd
almost say. But alive and *young,* and he looked like he
was going to do something marvelously *stupid* with

his life, like start a construction company and make lots of money. I could see him coming home in his dirty clothes. I could feel all the sweat and the gorgeous domestic *assumption*. I could hear him saying "What's for dinner, babe?" with his testicles in the words. *(Beat)* And I thought: that's the true, genuine life. To build and eat and screw and have children and die, and not waste a second reflecting on it, the way we do. *(She catches her breath at a particularly brilliant burst of fireworks.)*

(From the hallway, we can hear drunken song: HOMER.)

FRANK: God.

HOMER: *(From outside:)* Hark. What light through yonder window breaks? *(He opens the door.)* It is the east, and Frank is the sun. *(He enters, in full graduation splendor.)*

FRANK: Homer.

HOMER: It's me. Yes. Wandering the halls like a ghost. I wasn't invited to graduation, but I'll be damned if I'm going to miss it. Thirty three years I've sat on that stage. Wine? Is this wine? *(He pours himself a glass, flops in a chair, exhausted and already drunk.)* Hypocrites! Not a word from any of them, and they sat up there on that stage, extolling the virtues of humanism like it was so much stale cheese. Humanism. Not a one of them would know humanism if they tripped over it and broke their noses. It begins with the word "human", doesn't it? The individual, yes. Oh, speaking of individuals, this is rich, Frank. *(He begins digging in his pocket.)* I've found her name.

FRANK: *(Beat)* Whose name?

HOMER: The girl. Your girl's. *(Sings:)*
The girl I left behind
Sharon Ganz. I remembered. Yes. *(Still digging in his

pockets, but unable to find it.) I'll use it. I will certainly use it. Twenty years ago to this day, she would have graduated. I have her current address here. Marvelous, the usefulness of Mrs Plinth in the Alumni Office.

HEIDI: *(Confused)* Sharon Ganz? *(Then, recognition:)* Oh.

HOMER: *(Fumbling in his pocket)* And don't think. Don't think-. Where is it?

FRANK: There'll be no need to use it, Homer. Presuming the satisfactory completion of some unfinished business—we will be recommending to the President that, after a year's unpaid sabbatical, you be reinstated on a probationary basis.

(HOMER finds the paper He's been looking for.)

HOMER: That's the best they can do, then?

FRANK: Recommending to the President, yes. In another year, the student in question will have graduated. You'll, of course, be expected to undergo some therapy.

(FRANK can barely hide his distaste for the last. HOMER looks around.)

HOMER: A year's unpaid sabbatical. Reinstatement. *(He makes a decision, then rips up the paper in his hand.)* Here's what I'll do with this, then. The hell with Sharon Ganz. Go back where you came from. Ha! Ha! Thank you, Frank.

JACOB: I wouldn't rip that up so quickly if I were you.

HOMER: Why not?

JACOB: I haven't made up my mind yet, Frank.

(FRANK looks at JACOB, distressed. HOMER picks up on this.)

HOMER: What's this?

JACOB: Frank's been bargaining for my vote for his Ethnic Studies candidate, Homer. If I vote against a certain black academic, and in favor of the very white Miss Hopley, well, then he'll take care of you.

HOMER: I still don't understand.

JACOB: How can I explain?

HOMER: That seems hardly a choice at all. A no-brainer. Of course, hell, bring in a dozen Miss Hopleys. But save *me*.

(HEIDI *has been fixated on the ripped paper on the floor. Now she gathers it up, puts it together so that it is legible.*)

HEIDI: Sharon Ganz. She lives in Summitt, New Jersey, Frank. I'd totally forgotten her.

HOMER: *(Referring to* JACOB*)* So it's up to *him*, Frank?

FRANK: I'm afraid, yes.

HOMER: Well, Jacob, you can vote for this—

JACOB: I don't know if I can, Homer.

HEIDI: It's amazing that you can do that. Forget someone. Who was once, so important.

(HOMER *looking disbelievingly at* JACOB, *then making a dash for the paper in* HEIDI's *hands.*)

(*Holding the paper,* HOMER *picks up the phone.*)

MARGARET: I'm afraid I'm in the dark.

HEIDI: Frank got her pregnant twenty years ago.

MARGARET: And what happened?

HEIDI: We don't know. She went away. Did you keep in contact with her, Frank?

FRANK: I didn't. No.

HEIDI: (*Having greater difficulty containing what's going on inside of her.*) Did you know anything at all that happened to her?

FRANK: No, Heidi.

HEIDI: Did she have the child?

FRANK: I don't know, Heidi.

(HOMER *has dialed the number and been waiting.*
The connection is made.)

HOMER: Sharon Ganz? Homer Boykin.Yes. Yes. Hello.
How are you, dear? There's someone here who would
like very much to talk to you.

MARGARET: *(Mildly horrified)* You can't be doing this.

(HOMER *holds the phone out to* FRANK.)

HEIDI: Oh take it, Frank. Take it. Find out.

MARGARET: *(Steel)* Hang up now.

HOMER: *(Into phone)* Hold on, dear.

HEIDI: A child, or not a child?

MARGARET: Hang up. Don't torture that woman.

HEIDI: *(Desperate)* Frank.

(JACOB *goes over to the phone, takes it from* HOMER,
hangs it up, then yanks the cord out of the wall.)

JACOB: You're not going to do this.

HOMER: Oh, don't give me that. *He'll* stop at nothing.
He needs to be brought down.

JACOB: Maybe. Yes.

HOMER: Well, if not you, then who? Christ, if any
of you had any loyalty, any decent instinct for self-
preservation, you'd walk off this campus in protest.
I went over the line *once.* Where's forgiveness, hmm?
Where's the *human* here? Over the line *once,* after years
of abuse by men like *him.*

(JACOB *is sitting now.* HOMER *stands over him.*)

HOMER: What's all this about, Jacob? A *black* woman?
Do you think it makes any difference whether we have
one more black face on this campus, Jacob? What's that
going to make us? *(With distaste for the word:)* Inclusive?
Do you really think so? No. What we are goes deep,
Jacob. Change the colors of every face, we remain
a *white* institution. Now look me in the eye and tell
me that matters to you. This is me, Homer. Tell me
it matters. *(Beat)* Cut a deal. Cut—a deal.

JACOB: *(Beat)* No. I can't, Homer.

HOMER: *(Beat)* That's it, then? *(Beat. He sits heavily in
a chair, then, after a moment, bolts out of it, gathers hisrobes
about him, leaves.)*

FRANK: *(After a moment:)* There he goes. Thirty three
years he's been here, earning a very comfortable salary
for what amounts to very little work. Yet I'll wager he
sees something tragic in all this. *(Beat)* Heidi, it's getting
late.

HEIDI: I'm not going home with you, Frank.

FRANK: *(Beat)* I'll leave the side door open. In case you
change your mind.

HEIDI: Oh, I have my key for Christ's sake. Don't leave
the side door open. *(Beat)* I forgave you too easily,
Frank.

FRANK: *(More affected by this than he would like to let on.)*
Perhaps you did. But twenty years have gone by, Heidi.
You did forgive me once. *(Beat)* Well. I'll—nevertheless,
leave the side— *(He starts to go. Hesitates. As if he's
forgotten something.)* Well. goodnight. *(He goes.)*

(HEIDI at the window. In her own thoughts)

MARGARET: *(Careful, quiet)* There are worse things than
to be alone.

HEIDI: Are there? Perhaps for you. But for a woman like me? We gave ourselves away, that's what we did. Our generation. We didn't hold back. Not us. Not—me. More important than anything was to hold it together. You could never understand that, probably, the way we saw the world. *(Beat)* I did forgive him. *(Beat)* I'll take the long way home, I think. *(She goes.)*

*(*JACOB *and* MARGARET *alone.)*

MARGARET: Well. Bravo.

JACOB: No. Don't. Don't make it sound—honorable.

MARGARET: Why not? Christ. Does everything have to be shrouded in ambivalence?

(Beat. JACOB *looks at her a long moment.)*

JACOB: Yes. *(Beat)* Look, I just fucked over a decent man so that a black woman I don't even know can come here. Maybe that's the right thing to do, I'll grant you that, but let's not pretend we're standing on absolutes here.

MARGARET: Don't yell. It's okay. We don't even have to talk about it. I'll grant you license to always feel of two minds about everything you do. Just—come here. I don't want *tonight* to be about all this. *(But he doesn't come.)* Oh—what? What? *(Then, sensing it:)* Look, if this is what I think it is, I'd vastly prefer the way Aaron Goldman did it.

JACOB: I got out of bed last night. Out of your bed. I walked to my house. I stared up and I thought, here I am, a man supposedly in love and still I come here. Why? Staring up at my children's rooms, at my wife's—room. *Why?*

MARGARET: Because you are *crippled*. You are a man who can't make up his mind.

JACOB: *(Contained)* Let me do that, then. Let me make up my mind.

MARGARET: Listen to yourself. Asking permission.

JACOB: No. I'm like Heidi, I think. I gave myself away.

MARGARET: Part of yourself, maybe. And the other part is screaming to get out.

JACOB: Yes. But decisions have to be made.

(Beat. SHE senses that it is useless.)

MARGARET: So, back to the path. A little divergence. That was all this was.

JACOB: You know that's not true.

MARGARET: No. What was it then?

JACOB: I loved you.

MARGARET: All in the past then. Already.

JACOB: *(Beat)* I love you.

(She looks at him, trying to decide whether it's enough. JACOB's student, WENDY, bursts in, in her graduation robe.)

WENDY: He came! My Dad. My father. I'm sorry. Am I interrupting something?

MARGARET: No. No, you're not. *(Beat. To JACOB:)* Goodnight, then. *(She goes.)*

WENDY: *(Hard to contain her excitement.)* It's just— I never got a chance to thank you, or tell you— he's over at Willard's, waiting for me—leave it to him to pick the tackiest bar in town.

(Beat. JACOB is trying to control his emotions.)

WENDY: Are you okay?

JACOB: Yes.

WENDY: Just—completion, you know? He didn't tell me he was coming. There's hope. Don't let me make too much of it. This is just—everyone I deeply, deeply care about is sleeping in the same town tonight. I feel like I can protect them, that's all. For one night. *(Beat)* Goodbye.

JACOB: Wait. *(Beat)* I wanted to apologize. I didn't help. Forgive me.

WENDY: *(Beat. Composing her words carefully)* No. You—could have shown me more of your struggle, that's all. *(She exits.)*

(Beat. JACOB turns off his desk lamp. He goes and stands before the tall windows. Fireworks play across his face.)

(Then, someone at the door.)

(CHRIS enters, half-dressed and frantic. His shirt tail is out, his pants are stained and sweaty, he has been up for twenty four hours. He does not see JACOB.)

(CHRIS goes to his desk and removes, from where it was hidden, a bottle of champagne. He turns on his desk lamp, still does not see JACOB. He stands and opens the bottle, a little frantic in his movements. The cork pops, champagne bubbles up. He does not drink it. Instead, He pours it over his head, a baptism into his new, difficult life. Still, a moment of pure exultancy. Sounds coming from him, a mixture of ecstasy and pain. His hair, his shirt, his pants all gloriously soaked. Let him stand there. Let him have this moment. Then, He notices JACOB.)

CHRIS: *(Beat)* You're here.

JACOB: *(Beat)* Yes.

(Lights fade.)

END OF PLAY

www.ingramcontent.com/pod-product-compliance
Lightning Source LLC
Chambersburg PA
CBHW052205090426

42741CB00010B/2411